WARRIOR WOMAN

A Journal of My Life as an Artist

TINA LE MARQUE

Artists and Writers Press
Santa Fe, New Mexico

Additional copies of this book may be ordered through bookstores
or by sending $18.95 plus $2.50 for postage and handling to:
Publishers Distribution Service
121 E. Front Street, Suite 203
Traverse City, MI 49684
1-800-345-0096

Publisher's Cataloging-in-Publication Data

Le Marque, Tina, 1951-

    Warrior Woman : a journal of my life
    as an artist / Tina Le Marque. --Santa Fe, NM:
    Artists and Writers Press,
        p.   cm.
    ISBN 0-9630131-0-6
    1. Le Marque, Tina, 1951- 2. Women painters--United States--
Biography. 3. Painters--United States--Biography. I. Title.

ND37.L46L46   1992
759.13--dc20   91-73200

Manufactured in the United States of America

This book is dedicated with love to
my great husband, Bob Earll,
our magical kid, Sasha,
my Didi and Dad, my
precious Jeanne,
and to you,
fellow traveler,
full of fear and courage.

Tina Le Marque
Tucson, Arizona, 1991

About the Cover:

This painting, "Self Portrait in Transition," was painted in 1986, shortly before my departure from the City of the Angels, California. For some months before I painted this picture, I intuitively knew that an avalanche of change was about to sweep through my happy life. I had no idea what form that change was going to take. I just knew that things didn't "feel right" where I was any more.

Upon exiting from my shower one evening, I looked at myself in the mirror. I caught one truly horrifying fleeting glimpse of my face, ravaged by exhaustion and confusion. The starkness and honesty of that face prompted me to look again, even though I didn't want to. What I saw in the mirror was almost more than even I could bear to look at. I saw a woman shredded by her own emotions. I saw the face of a woman falling into the abyss. I saw myself in a state of utter disintegration. I rushed to the storeroom for a canvas.

I painted this painting weeping and breaking, with my left hand, although I am right-handed, in a room almost dark in the falling twilight. I did not turn on the light for fear the vision would flee. In a state of waking dreaming, I worked as quickly as I could. All the pain is there in the painting, and all the terror. I saw mystery there as well, along with potent symbols of my own healing and strength, even through the collapse I knew was coming.

I don't usually explain too much about my work. People project all their own stuff onto artists' work, and I prefer to let that process go on without any assistance or interference from me. But it seemed necessary to put out some words about this powerful vision. The face in this painting became a beacon for me. She became my Warrior Woman, who would lead me through magical means and paths unseen by most people, to a new life. My terror and my faith were absolute as I put my hand in her's and jumped over the edge.

Foreword

Usually when people write a foreword they write about the book, but in this instance I would rather write about the woman who wrote the book. She is perhaps one of the most remarkable women I have known. I've read the book and the back cover and some of the ads. They talk about her zest for life, the great lengths she goes to and has gone to for personal and creative freedom, a warrior woman. What they fail to mention is that this warrior woman whose need for personal and creative freedom has driven her like a jet engine wants those she loves to experience the same freedom.

I have watched for three years and three months, while she has created a safe and loving environment for her daughter to enjoy those freedoms, without it having to be a struggle, a war. Occasionally her daughter will stand there and shout "I hate you." I watch as Tina processes the hurt with the knowledge that she has created a space in which her child can express herself without fear of punishment or without fear of love being withheld. I daily get to experience the power of a home where a three year old has the power that her mother had to fight for years to acquire. I get to see this child paint and draw where no one insists she stay within the lines or that grass has to be green.

A few weeks ago we were in Mexico at a Club Med and I watched as this child carefully picked the councilor she was going to use for her personal caretaker. Sure enough for the next week they were practically inseparable. A child who knows how to go about creating as safe an environment as possible while she tries to figure out this adventure called life.

I am father to that child and husband to that mother. I too am a writer and have supported myself as such for twenty three years. The first twenty years were spent writing television and let me tell you I had a few things to learn about the value of my work from Tina. I would constantly tell her I thought she was asking too much money for her paintings, or that she should paint what people were buying. Lovingly and patiently she helped me see that my work had value, that the fact I had supported myself creatively was a great and wondrous thing. She was there for me when I wrote and published my first book encouraging me to write what I had to say, what I wanted to say and not worry about others. She encouraged me to be true to me. She was passing on to me gifts that she had won in battle.

I have listened as she has spent hours upon hours on the phone with friends listening, sharing as they struggled to find their place. She shares unselfishly of what she has found. She has deeply touched the lives of many people in her short time here on earth.

I don't believe critics serve a useful purpose. They create nothing, they rely on others to do the work first. It's as if in their arrogance they think the rest of us need them to figure out whether or not something is good or bad. So I won't be saying this is a good book or a bad book but I will tell you it was written by a woman who has overcome the horrors of being raised by two alcoholics, the downward spiral of her own addiction and the lies of a society bent on controlling the human spirit, to become a loving, giving, witty, spontaneous, risk taking, thirty nine-year-old woman that women everywhere can be proud of. I encourage you to share her adventure. I have for four and a half years and it has been mystical, magical and wondrous...

Bob Earll

Contents

So now for the benefit of myself and all the other creative outsiders I am going to start allowing it to pour out, just as it always has poured out. I have chosen the form of a journal, because it is most suited to the kind of creating that I do — very stream of consciousness. I plan to let you inside the life of an artist. I will honestly tell you the story of my feelings, my fears, my struggles, my successes, what I have learned and what I am learning now.

Chapter 1

THE RUSTY GATES OPEN
I begin to write again . . . Life in the concrete jungle . . .
My teachers . . . Notes on my process . . .

July 23,1986
"The Artist as Shaman"

All day long I have been thinking about those words. I wanted to write them down some place, maybe think about them later. After a few hours they started to annoy me. I wanted to forget about them. I didn't want to have to find a pen that works — a clean piece of paper. So after thinking about where the pen might be, what the words mean to me, now I can't stop thinking of the phrase. It's like an annoying commercial I've inadvertently picked up from TV. After trying every avoidance technique, now it's the middle of the night and I can't sleep. I'm the kind of writer who, after setting the alarm for six in the morning to get ready for an important interview that I really care about, is suddenly wide awake, without a chance in hell to get any sleep at all that night. NO! The *artiste* inside of me wants to work right now. Sleep be damned! It's time to sit down to the empty page, the long hours of a sleepless night. I've also been trying to avoid writing this thought-provoking little phrase down because I know that if I allow myself to start writing there will be many, many sleepless nights in my future. First a trickle will come, then a torrent. I will be in danger of the whole dam breaking. I hope I'll be able to stop once in awhile to blow my nose. Better stock up on Earl Grey. With caffeine.

Writing is like that for me — but I am a *bruja*, a shamaness, a high priestess in the world of art. I eat sacred earth whenever available and I time the start and finish of my projects by the phases of the moon. I wear bracelets of lizards and earrings of snakes. I am a changer, a trickster, a coyote in a coat of many colors. I am the rattler camouflaged in the dead cholla wood by your feet. I am a child of the stars and I live in the dreamtime. Much that I put my hand to is sacred or becomes so to me, but I am just as comfortable rolling up my sleeves and sloshing through the poop and the mud. Just the same, if I try to put this off any longer, the magic might vanish, turning in on me, against me. If I wait until it is a good time, until I am ready to start a book, the bomb may have gone off, the volcano erupted. My life might alter so drastically that I won't be able to write. I have something inside of me that needs to be said. I'll have to just start now because the book is starting on me. Might as well get up and face the dragon.

3

This is how all of my favorite work has come out — with urgency. Suddenly I know that my life depends upon it. The secret to the demanding creative outpouring which has at times been so frightening to me, has only been that I have shown up, according to my own call of the wild. It is a voice soft at first, but insistent — "Get up and work. You're not sleeping tonight — or any other night — until you face this."

When I first started painting I went to the studio once a week. Gradually, my ability to concentrate increased. I became capable of working more, so I made a commitment to paint twice a week. I resisted, held back a little — not much. I wondered if maybe I would be better off — better adjusted — if I were working in a hamburger stand or a drugstore like my friends. I was afraid that this inner call would kidnap me from the living. When I got going, quit holding back, really started adventuring into the world of making art, what actually happened was that it made me more available to life. It gave me more sensors to feel with. The colors became more vivid, the music more inviting, the dance more sinuous and full of mystery. Who wouldn't want more?

For a long time I criticized myself because I needed to go to someone else's studio to work. If I were a "real artist" I should be able to do it all alone. I should find a nice rat turd-filled garret and move in with nothing but my art supplies, a bare light bulb and some cockroaches. I was eighteen when I took the fork in the road that said "Artists (fools) go this way." I didn't know how to draw. Like everyone in the U.S. of A., I had used crayons and some crummy paints of the brand they dole out so carefully, as if they were gold, in grade school. At eighteen, I was afraid to go to the life-drawing class where the models would be wearing no clothes. When I drew, the models looked weird. Like extra terrestrials, maybe, you know — the drawings they have in the National Inquirer of the little people who sucked the old couple from Iowa up into their spaceship. The people I drew had arms that looked kind of funny and stringy. My drawing teacher taught me not to make little potato-shapes at the end of their legs — to take the time to really look — to draw the toes, go all around the toenails, follow and draw every little crease and lump as if I were running my hand over the model's skin.

There was one model I drew early on who weighed upwards of two hundred pounds. She was covered in quivering cellulite from ankles to hair roots. No wonder so many people squirm at the thought of drawing from a naked model! I had to go outside and have what amounted to a therapy session with my instructor before I could face her behind. When the instructor moved the stand she was modelling on (I don't know how...), he fell a little, and his right hand plunged deep into her fat, blubbery belly. I almost threw up. I wondered what my parents would think if they could see this fat woman. Eeek! What was this warped new world I had entered?

In another drawing group, an uninstructed lab, there was a goony guy who I noticed was sitting right in front of the model's spread-eagle legs. I soon noticed that he moved his chair directly in front of her crotch each time she shifted into a new position. Perhaps he was studying for gynecological text renderings? And she? In every pose she more and more resembled a person who had ridden a horse once too often. As she sprawled more or less in my direction, he swooped into position for a good close up of her labia. I observed some little stick figures on his sketch pad... such are the courtships unique to the art world.

Anyway, it's time now to return to writing. I've been painting full time, making like a professional for over fifteen years. I got lost in the paint. It gave me a longer leash to participate out in the world and the river of life than writing seemed to. When I would give in to the urge to write, I would write and write and write and write and write and write. I couldn't wait to make a break for it to go out and get drunk — have some fun!

I didn't want to be locked up with a typewriter, out of the sunlight, musing, dripping in angst. I clutched my pain to me when I wrote. I didn't want to live at that level. I wanted to be singing, dancing, flying through the air, not connected to an electric cord. Besides — when I started writing there were no computers. I was a hopeless typist. I could never stay awake long enough to get through a single typing class. My pages were full of white-out. Even now I always have a bottle in my purse.

The bottom line is that I get my life assignments from a higher source. The more I've worked for this employer, the more wonderful and weirder my life has become. As I go along my own unique path I seem to exercise less and less control. Like a lightning bolt, change and adventure come into my life. There is no such thing as an ordinary day. In the last few years I have had to follow the most individual, lonely, puzzling and convoluted path, following the little voice inside of me. You know, the one that says, "You can't keep doing what you're doing right now." I've had to walk out — under a compulsion to do so from what seemed to me to be a perfectly good marriage — out of The Mansion. It drove me crazy, looking for answers about why I had to do that. I moved from an estate into what amounted to a chicken coop in the barrio in Santa Monica. My life became harder, but I mysteriously became happier, freer.

Still it has plagued me — why, why, why? During that first year after I left my husband I lived in a trailer, my car, the chicken coop with my dog. I ran Felicity House, a recovery home in L.A. for strange women who were escaping alcohol and drug addiction, as I had done myself eight years before. I painted at night in Dorothy Cannon's studio — bless her, she saved my being from oblivion. I took a tremendous amount of comfort from reading the biographies, autobiographies, hearsay and articles about people who had had to walk away from the conveyor belt themselves — Henry Miller, Anais Nin, Georgia O'Keefe. It made me feel as if I weren't the only misfit. For several weeks, each time I picked up the phone it would be someone asking me about some new piece of juicy gossip they had just heard about me, how my life was falling apart, what a loser I my husband was saying I was. The life stories of these other artists and writers gave me the courage to continue to feel my way down the unlit hallways of my life. I may have been crying and terrified, but I was going forward. Fast.

At this time, July of 1986, I have been a full-time artist for about seventeen years . I've been a dedicated journal keeper since I was given my first red diary with a tiny, fragile gold lock when I was a small girl, somewhere around age seven. I started working at it very honestly and in earnest. There was a lock on the diary—it was to be filled with treasure. The need to express myself to others has always been pressing. I grew up in a 100% alcohol and drug addicted family. There was serious violence and drunkenness in my home from long before the time when Christina Ann Webster (That's one of me!) was conceived. Through-out my childhood, until age 24, I was extremely ill from asthma. I lived like a cripple, unable to ride a bike or run with other kids. I became addicted to prescription drugs shortly after I began taking them — serious prescription drugs, particularly for a five-year old. I was a chronic drug-induced insomniac, totally nuts at night, pathologically lonely and alone. I needed someone to talk to, and I had the little red diary. Journal keeping is a habit, a relationship. I needed someone to talk to and the little red book with the golden lock was always there. I wore the key on a ribbon around my neck. Now it's maybe thirty years later. I'm still writing in my journal! It's one of the longest, healthiest relationships I've had. Journal keeping has also been the little gold key to my relationship with myself — the key to unlocking the pain that came as a result of growing up in a very interesting, but really sick, family. I know I need to record this stuff — the blood and guts and magic of my life. My emotional involvement with my journal has been a gift. A gift of pain, a gift of learning.

In art, it's one thing to study, to learn a technique. There's a drive to create —usually pretty strong, even if it's underground. The drive can carry you along in your work, keep you going forward, if you can get out of the way and let it. Sounds so easy when I say it that way. But getting your work out there where people can see it, that's another story. It is far more challenging to develop the means to give the product away — and by this I certainly don't mean to literally give the work away. I mean to share it — put it where people can see it, finger it, touch it, smell it. It's important to get paid, too. Artists need to get their work out where people can see it as much as they need to do their art.

Art is about communicating. If we can find a way to put a little of what we have been given as creative people back into the river of life, our own lives are somehow just a little richer, the colors in our world become a little brighter. I often think how hard life is in certain passages, and what a gift it is to have art, music, all the great books available to us. It makes the rocky parts a little more endurable. With art, either as creators or as pleasure-takers, there is more to our lives than just the current squirmy, contagious stuff under the microscope.

These days the river of life seems polluted to anyone who has the guts to look at it. The soul of the earth is becoming harder and harder to find. The artist is a healer. Creative people have the ability to gather and shake up all the wild forces of life, of growth, of the human spirit, and pour this magical cocktail back into the river. That is my job as an artist. That is why the most important thing I can do in my life is create; not imitate, create.

So when this phrase/epithet/epitaph, "The Artist as Shaman," came to me today, although I am tired it seemed that today was a good day to give in to the urge to sit down and write. Some people do okay in life starting tomorrow — not me. If I wait before I create, every moment spent delaying diminishes some of the force, the desire. Pretty soon the whole idea has a way of just floating down the crapper. I'll just make the bed first. Then I've got to go to the market...

When I work around other people it isn't long before I catch them with their mouths hanging open. I work fast. Really fast. It gushes out into the room. My method is simple: I get out of the way. I'm a channel for the creative force. The more I get out of the way, the more comes out. When the itch comes, I sit down and scratch, more or less wherever I am. If I'm having, say, a dinner party, and I get some images overlapping the thrilling repartee, I don't wait until the dinner party is over. I make some sketches on the place mat or anything at hand. No need to be polite or shy — people expect artists to be self-centered jerks. Most people actually like to just sit there with you while you spout art. I don't wait until I'm not tired or it's convenient for my partner or 'til I've got time.

Also, when I have had to work straight jobs, I painted in the evening. I was very tired during the day — tired, but I was an artist, not just a receptionist at a beauty shop with fluorescent lights, or the exec director for a recovery home full of extremely peculiar, delightfully brilliant, but demanding young working women. I was first and foremost an artist, and it was essential for the quality of my life that I keep on actively doing my art, even under distracting or even discouraging circumstances. Art is fun for me; jobs are not. Anyway, I make sure there is always a time and place for my art. The world will have to run itself without my help when it is time for me to paint. I used to tell the troops at Felicity House that they had better not choose Wednesdays to commit suicide or get arrested, because I was going

7

to the studio to paint and I wouldn't be showing up to cut them down from the rafters until I was done.

In the straight working world I often heard people talking about the things they would do when they had time, when they could afford it, when they didn't have social obligations. I gave up sleeping so that I could paint. When I worked, the first money I set aside after rent and food was for art lessons and supplies. In other words, I put my art in the category of a necessity. I also gave up social obligations. Artists can't afford to be obligated, socially or otherwise.

What it boiled down to for me was that without my art, I had no life. Jobs came and went. So did money. Men came and went even faster. For some time in my young womanhood my feelings about myself were on a seesaw, with these ever-shifting commodities on the other end. When I changed jobs or men, I lost any feeling of well-being. I gradually learned in desperation to turn to the easel in times of emotional upheaval to reconnect with a stabilizing force. My art, that was a faithful friend and lover. When I was lonely, the paints and the journal were always there. Art could be my comfort at all times, day or night. This became even more important when I gave up alcohol and drugs. The feelings were big and getting bigger. There was no other place to express them in the middle of the night.

When I came to the studio empty, I was filled up again by painting. When life dealt its shattering blows, art was my healer. When I was lost I painted the darkness and all the things I feared. My art gave me an outlet for my tidal wave-sized feelings. Through painting I was able to give form and even faces to the disconnected and often warring parts of myself. More than once I stayed alive to paint the state of my being when all I wanted to do was die. And I did know how to die. Living was another matter altogether. That would take some learning.

I first learned to find my feelings and express them through writing. It seemed then that it demanded more and more of me, requiring that I write out every word, every nuance of my life. It was too inward, sometimes, too self-obsessed, finally. I never could stop long enough to go out and live. Something would happen and I would have to go home and write about it. When I began painting it solved that dilemma for me. I was looking out at my subjects, at least a lot of the time in the beginning years, to learn the technique. I was lucky enough to land in the middle of art teachers who knew about therapy, art therapy, and the unconscious. They were able to guide me on the journey inward — "Now paint it," they would say! "What did you dream last night? Now paint that with your left hand." It was a little inside, a little outside — a healing balance for me. I had a lot to tell, and I could say it all so much quicker with a brush in each hand!

Even now as I write it holds some fear. I will have to live at this god-damned computer. But the painter is well-entrenched now. Shapes, colors, forms and movement have anchored me into this reality, even as I drift into other worlds. I used to take tranquilizers by the handful just to slow my mind down enough so that I could keep up with the writing. I also needed valium to make myself hold still in one place long enough to work.

So now for the benefit of myself and all the other creative outsiders I am going to start allowing it to pour out, just as it always has poured out. I have chosen the form of a journal because it is most suited to the kind of creating that I do — very stream of consciousness. I plan to let you inside the life of an artist. I will honestly tell you the story of my feelings, my fears, my struggles, my successes, what I have learned and what I am learning now.

July 24, 1986

The people who have most helped me get to where I am right now are a large Fellini-like troupe of artists, writers, dancers, therapists, and jugglers who have gone before, holding a match in the dark. There was Dorothy Royer, Dorothy Cannon, Sueo Serisawa, Arnold Schifrin, Jane Manning. I am the artist I am today because of many years of study in their studios.

How lucky I was to have been led to each of these teachers! And there was the other person who was so important — the one who stepped out of the shadows where I found myself wanting to die, and taught me how to live, how to even want to live. That's Jeanne. Jeanne who? Hah! There's only one. Without her I would not have stayed alive long enough to write this journal. I met her in 1975 in the bushes outside a meeting where I was trying to get help for my bizarre and deadly drinking. She taught me that all human beings have the same set of feelings, whether they are aware of or able to be honest about them.

Because of my experiences with Jeanne I know that there are other people like me out there who need to know "It can be done." She made me aware that there is a world full of people who feel like I do — who struggle; who don't think they can do what they are meant to do because they don't think they have a right to do so. There are many people who are afraid to show their work to anyone because nobody would like it or even care. They may not let their feelings hang out in the wind for everyone to see like I have to, but the feelings are just the same as mine.

There are plenty of other people who are just "stuck," not doing their life's work. When the artist is not doing her or his art, they are dying inside, a little bit every day. Artists are either busy creating or busy destroying. Like most people, our flair for destruction far exceeds our ability or desire to create, and we are generally much more dramatic about the staging of it all. In fact you might say that when we get into a full-scale downslide it takes on the proportions of a Cecil B. De Mille production. Big. Flashy. Lots of people go over the cliff with the heroine/hero... surprising thing is, though, we all get to decide. It's do your art or die inside... no big deal. You decide.

I'll write more later. I'm sorry that the full moon is past. I usually try to time the beginning of a new project when the moon is new. The waning phase is for finishing projects... a primitive system, pagan even. Works okay for the tides though. However, this project demanded that I start tonight. All I did was show up, wild-eyed, sleepless and pale as a true daughter of the moon.

Chapter 2

THE JOURNEY BEGINS
Los Angeles . . . Teaching . . . "The Nothing" . . . Creative binge . . .
The harvest celebration . . . Dance Home . . .

July 26, 1986

It has taken me three days to recover from opening the rusty gates to the writing. I have been consumed thinking, thinking, thinking. When I start writing, it is like that. When I drive down the street thoughts assault me with such fury that I have to keep a pen and index cards in the truck. I write as I drive. Sometimes I pull over and write like a sane person. But if there is any business to be done in the outside world, I must simply try to not slam into other cars while I scrawl my ideas. I imagine the neighboring drivers must be delighted to find themselves next to someone who is writing on their steering wheel, laughing wildly all by herself or weeping disconsolately.

About a year and a half ago I started on my current painting binge. One of my collectors had bought a group of paintings. It was the biggest sale I'd ever made. I looked around his house and saw originals by Picasso and Chagall. He and his wife had previously purchased a painting he had seen at my home shortly after my separation from Philippe. This was a couple that just loved art. They chose three of my best pieces. I realized then that it had been a long time since I had painted anything of great emotional or artistic significance. None of my work had sent me reeling toward the back wall. I had been piddling.

After a complete physical and emotional collapse a dear friend, Kelly, picked me up and brushed me off. He allowed me the opportunity to quit my straight job and just do my art. A great post-dirty divorce healing took place then because I was able to do just what I was supposed to do — make art. I could wallow in purple and turquoise and blue and pink. The colors healed me in the places that no-one else could reach.

The combination of utter defeat and selling those three paintings set off the most artistically productive period in my life. I came to regard my current collapse in a different way. It was the difficulty in my life that started the pain inside of me that drove me to surrender to doing my art, to creating. I had no place left to go. Oddly enough, most artists and creative people will go to great lengths to avoid doing the very thing that brings us the most relief, pleasure and fulfillment — our art.

At the point when I knew I would have to quit my job in the recovery home or die I got into my car with my German shepherd, Chile Bean, and we went out into a deserted canyon in the Santa Monica Mountains. All my life I had been trying to side-step disaster. Now my collapse was about to turn into an ally.

11

Chile and I sat down under a favorite oak tree, in the center of an oak grove. The tiny flame inside of me was just about out. It felt like I had been beaten by everything and everybody. I was burned-out by my job. I had destroyed my seemingly happy marriage and already lost interest in the illusion I had left to chase. Friendships of many years standing had exploded like landmines. There was no safe place to go except inside of myself.

Out in the safety of the oak grove I panicked, as disappointment and depression wrapped darkly around me, closing off the exits and the air vents. From way inside a desperate and confused voice came: "What can I do to help myself heal? I'll do anything." An answer came from inside and outside myself, "Just let it heal. That's all. Just let it." We stayed there as the evening fell, so we could leave in the protection of the darkness as quietly as we came. I couldn't stand the pain of people's eyes on my skin.

Over the next few months one big painting after the other forced its way out, down my arms, through my hands. I stood back, with a sense that the work was coming through me. The less effort on my part, the more the paintings flowed out.

One of the paintings I worked on at this time was a painting of Century City, a magazine-slick development west of Beverly Hills. If you drive west on Olympic Boulevard to go to the beach, you will see the exact view. Cold-hearted monoliths rising up at crazy angles on a hillock. There is an oil derrick which someone was considerate enough to cover, so as not to offend. It's a developer's Stonehenge, the covert insult of the 20th century. When I grew up in Beverly Hills it was just like a cozy little village. We all grew more and more morose every time another one of those skyscrapers went up because it took another piece of the sky, stole another chunk of the sunset or the stars. So this painting was somehow a recognition of this atrocity. There is a stream of little cars (automaton-omobiles) and non-humans walking at the bottom of the piece. I call it "The Slum-Dwellers." I used all the colors that make me feel better — violets, strangled pinks, city-shadow blues. I took my small black sketch book and a little Pentel brush-pen I get a good line with, and found the spot where I needed to be to get the sketch down for the painting I would do next. I had to stop dead in the middle of the boulevard, put my sketch book on the steering wheel and paint as fast as I could. Then a big rush of traffic would bear down on me and I'd have to drive around the block. Lucky I didn't feel the urge to actually paint the picture right there in the road.

I had to come around to the same spot in the road four or five times. The eccentricity, the impracticality of it, gave me the feeling I was really an artist. I think that all artists need to do things that are ridiculous, impractical — even dangerous sometimes. We need to push out the boundaries of what is acceptable behavior in our society. Deep inside, in my cells, I am an adventuress, and this was a time in my life when a lot of adventures were taking place.

There is something I need to do now to help me incubate my next painting. Yesterday I was reading an article and the word "Sphinx" came into my mind. I made myself quiet inside and floated across the void. Suddenly an enormous painting, at least five feet by seven feet came into my vision. I see a woman lying on the sands in Egypt. There are pyramids in the background, and the Sphinx. I sense she is a new and also very ancient part of my self. Her wings are upraised. She is ready to take flight, and she is shedding her skin which no longer fits her. All around her are golden snakes collecting and storing knowledge as they swim in the sand.

In our culture people have been programmed to have an automatic recoiling or fearful reaction to snakes. As a child, my reluctant mother allowed me to associate with our crawling relatives, and even let me have a snake as a pet although she no longer visited me in my room. I wasn't afraid of snakes and most of the rest of the world was so they were fellow outsiders and seemed liked friends to me. Snakes, as storers of the knowledge of the earth, frighten away those who fear the snake in themselves. This was instinctively apparent to me as a small child. Their presence provided me with some natural kind of protection from squeamish adults.

The Chumash Indians of California believed that there were two snakes who held up the crust of the earth. They were not negative entities. When they became tired they shifted, causing earthquakes. I often find myself in strange encounters with snakes. I am both mesmerized by them and reassured by their presence. They are medicine for me.

I am wrestling with this because there is not enough space in my studio to produce, hang or store another large piece. Really I would prefer to make it six feet by eight feet. So I am putting out that notification to the cosmos that I need help. There is something that I need to do, and no place to do it.

There is another painting simmering inside of me called "The Funeral of the Artist" which I am dying to do. It's also a monster-sized job. Why don't I just buy a museum? I need to so everyone can see this stuff... the painting is the story of the death and transformation/ resurrection of the Self through the process of leaving an old life and finding a new one. Perhaps the Source that keeps sending me all these urgent images would be so kind as to locate some extremely large, cheap, well-lit place to work.

July 28, 1986

There is an old saying: When the teacher is ready, the student arrives. One of the most exciting, frightening, risky, gratifying things that I have done in my art life is to begin teaching. At first, it seemed an outlandish idea, like most of the best things in life. Some friends came asking for lessons. I said 'no' a few times, until it became obvious that I was supposed to say 'yes'. When I am dealt five aces it usually occurs to me that I should bet on the aces.

I hadn't the slightest idea about how to go about teaching anything. I rushed to the bookstore and the library. I checked out Nicholaide's *The Natural Way to Draw*. I crashed through *Drawing on the Right Side of the Brain*. I bought books on teaching children to draw and paint. I worried at every opportunity.

I stayed awake, thinking about what a mistake I had made in saying yes. Shortly all these expectant and enthused friends would know how incompetent I really was. I would stumble over my words, like I always do when I am nervous. I would sweat, not perspire. I wouldn't know what to tell them to do if they finished too quickly or if they lost interest. The bottom line was really that I had no experience and no right to teach. Except there were these students sitting there in my studio...

I decided to teach by working on my own projects while the students were working on theirs. It seemed as if the sum of the two people struggling in the studio side-by-side had a generating effect. There was more power for both of us to draw from. One of the things I feared was that having students would drain me, would take me from my own work, syphon off my creative drive. The experience I had was just the opposite. The more I taught, the more I painted. The more I painted, the more I wanted to paint.

I had learned to paint in the studios of other practicing artists, rather than going to traditional art school. I was easily bored and always worked best in an unconventional, hands-on learning mode. Unusual and inspiring teachers who also worked and lived outside of the mainstream were not too hard to find. In fact learning how to find such teachers became a big part of my art education. In this way I planned my own course of study and answered to no-one but myself. I chose my teachers carefully, for their ability to bring out what was inside of me, without imposing their own images, opinions and standards. I didn't have to conform to anyone else's ideas of what was good art. I didn't paint for grades. I couldn't anyway.

This all sounds a little lofty, but I was such a rebel and a misfit that I didn't have any other choice. What I wanted to learn about and to do had nothing to do with what I was seeing turned out from the universities or art schools. In fact I seemed to value everything the traditional school system did not. I rarely saw work in galleries that I liked. Much of the popular, saleable art seemed flat, lifeless. It was technically good or even very good, but it still seemed without feeling. I didn't identify with the artists, I didn't fit in the art world. I couldn't go to school with these people. It would have been waste of tuition. I didn't want to make their kind of art anyway.

As I went along my way in the world I felt more and more respect for the teachers I met who were working off the safe path. When I began to teach I chose to try to use the same methods by which I was taught. I received a great deal of help and encouragement from the teacher I stayed with the longest, Dorothy Cannon. It was almost reassuring when she told me I could do it. Frequently I thought with horror about what I was setting out to do. I would run to Dorothy's art-filled house/sanctuary in panic and ask her what to do, what to say, where to start. She gave me herb tea and told me I could do it! Then she would hand me a paint brush and some paper...

I am writing all of this in detail because I know there are other people out there who would like to leave their boring jobs and don't believe it is possible to make it as an artist. That's what everyone tells you from the word go. You can't make it as an artist. It is my job to contradict that mistaken, non-threatening piece of misinformation, to tell you, hoping it will totally tear apart your life as you know it: You can make it as an artist. It probably won't be an easy life. But you have an obligation to yourself and to life to try to do so!

The desire to create in any field is a gift. There is an obligation that goes with that gift. You must use it and you must find a way to give it back to the world.

This morning at 9:30 a.m. I was out in the mists in the hills above Los Angeles. Two adventurous students and I were out for a Sunday morning painting trip. It was cold and damp. We were seeking comfort in a thermos of strong honey and mint tea. It was dreary and the location didn't willingly reveal its beauty or its secrets. We would have to work alongside a road travelled fairly frequently by cars, which I didn't like.

We usually work out under some trees in an out of the way, semi-wild spot. Everyone brings their dogs along with their drawing and painting supplies. The more they become accustomed to painting outdoors, the lighter they travel. Generally, they start by bringing oils on the backs of camels and llamas. After carting all their debris around a few times they get onto the idea that it would be great to paint with watercolors. Or maybe even the end of a twisted stick and some mud.

When we arrive at our site, we dump everything on the ground, just like this morning. We spread out some drop cloths and lie down or get into a meditative position for five to ten minutes. I like to rest my back up against a tree to gather its energy for painting. I love to paint trees, and it's good to talk to one before you paint its picture. Actually this idea came to me because I was having such incredible anxiety attacks at finding myself out with people who were expecting me to know what I was doing. I found that the only way to calm the attacks of fear was to hold still for a few moments and return to my body. Slowing down, I could plug into the healing power of nature. I could harness the energy to paint.

15

WARRIOR WOMAN

Before beginning our work we listen to the birds, the wind, the stream — all the things people miss when they are living/dying in this giant over-crowded rabbit warren called Los Angeles. If all my artists did when they came out in nature to paint was to lay on the ground and listen to the birds, it would be invaluable to their art. The ability to live in the present moment is the greatest gift any artist can have.

I like to lie on my back and look up at the leaves, the branches, the light flickering everywhere. If there is running water nearby, I'm in paradise.

Once everyone has caught her breath and slowed their poor little jangled minds down enough to actually see something, we begin to draw. Everyone finds something that calls to them and brings it back to the circle to draw.

We do contour drawings for about fifteen minutes. It seems to take a little time to access the right brain. I find that if we leave out the contour drawing ritual I cannot get them over the various interior obstacles that prevent them from getting work they are satisfied with.

Then everyone goes off in their separate directions to find whatever it is that has drawn them out early on a cold and damp Sunday morning. Throughout the morning I travel from painter to painter, stopping to work with each of them, or just to watch them in their own process.

I mostly like to draw on these excursions. After working on several drawings from the outside world I very often get an image for a large piece. I do small black and white sketches of these. Right now I'm using a 5"x7" bound sketchbook and my Pentel brush pen (brush tip, not a sponge tip).

The sketches I did for some of my Tarot series came in this way. The Empress appeared in an oak grove where I was drawing trees, enchanted by their branches. Now she is on a 4'x6' canvas in what used to pass as my living room. I can have tea with her whenever I want in my studio. She likes it there. Everyone does.

After our painting time we all gather together for tea, apples, cheese and crackers. Everyone puts their work up against the trees. Then I ask them to talk about what they've done, what happened for them. They tell what they like, what they didn't like, what they want to work on. They share their frustrations and their breakthroughs. The process and the end product are equally important.

I usually comment briefly on their pieces, but it seems that the words of a teacher carry more importance than they should. I feel my main purpose as a teacher is to provide a safe, productive atmosphere and a good example of a working artist. My next task is to get them out there painting. I am very careful in any criticism I might give. It's essential to hear what they have to say, and invaluable for them to learn to talk about their process and identify their feelings about their work.

Brief talk of this kind is often the key to unlocking long-barricaded doors to creativity. People need to tell their secrets about their art. Not too much verbally, though. Better to quickly steer them back to expressing their feelings through their artistic medium. I usually can find a pretty non-intrusive way to help open up their blind spots when we work over long periods of time. You can't get beyond the gauntlet of inner art critics with one visit to art class or a weekend workshop. I like to do this in as subtle a way as possible, respecting the student's own vision, which may be quite different from my own. I want them to end up with their taste, not mine. I want their paintings to look like their paintings, not like mine or anyone else's.

I don't like copy work for students. Most people have their own great storehouse of creativity. It's best to help them locate the path to it right away. Some people will be forever copiers. They don't interest me — it's the originals in people and art that I'm looking for.

July 31, 1986

Today I am in the Nothing. It is a place I drop into where I am nothing, I do nothing, I don't have any desire to do anything.

I don't want to paint, to ride a horse fast like the wind, or to go to the gym. I do not want to be an artist or an anything else. The Nothing wraps itself around me like a stupor. I am Nothing. I fall into the hole or I jump off the cliff, it depends. The result is the same: I drop into an abyss of lethargy and inertia.

The first time I fell into the Nothing in my creative life, I decided I had better paint what I thought was my last painting. It was a painting of two women from inside of me, talking heatedly. They were angry, angry, angry. They looked angry in the painting. I gave the painting away to someone who had always encouraged my art. It was to be my last; I was no longer a painter.

When the Nothing overtakes me I'm sure I'll never paint again. My brain becomes thick with goo. Images don't come. Words come with great difficulty. The first time I fell into the nothing I couldn't talk about it — I didn't know what it was. I didn't even know if it was there or not. It wasn't a depression, but it settled down on top of my energy source like one.

It used to be a frightening place for me, but as the years have gone by it has lost its fearsomeness. It seems to run its course, and after examining the Nothings I finally concluded that they were healthy. It is a time of recharging, of incubation, an essential turn in the spiral of my creative cycle — the one that ultimately brings me to the next round of intense creative activity. But in the Nothing I don't care about any of this. In the Nothing I'm a grease spot or less. It's a relief!

At the moment I believe my creative power is gathering force, like a hurricane, turning in upon itself, building velocity, before it breaks out loose upon a disempowering world. It leaves me on edge. It's the feeling before a thunderstorm. Something needs to happen to break the tension.

There are a number of paintings working their way up to the surface. At this moment in time, the need to push them out has not reached full force. Now I'm drifting in a Dead Sea of nothing. There is nothing that I can do or want to do to facilitate or accelerate the process. I am emptiness. I am nothingness. I am a womb, waiting. But when the time comes to do my work, it won't matter any more that the studio is completely full, the garage is overflowing, that the images are too big, that there is no place to put them, no gallery, maybe months with no buyer. Nothing will matter, except birthing the work.

I am looking at my Lunar Calendar, which I live by. The moon is waning. It explains some of the nothingness. It will continue to lose power until the 5th of August, when it will be No Moon. On August 6th there will be a New Moon. That is when I will focus my energies to begin working again.

Tomorrow is August Eve. August Eve is the celebration of Harbondia, the Goddess of Plenty. It also honors the Indian Corn Mothers, the full harvest. My harvest has been astonishing this year — there's much to celebrate. It is a day of fullness to overflowing. I plan to spend it with the Empress, the last Tarot card/painting I have completed. It is her day — a day of abundance and fertility.

The Empress is holding court in the studio at the moment. She was a difficult card for me to complete, to identify with, representing great fulfillment, fertility. Fertility is a frightening force to me, other than in my art. I identify with the Empress on the creative level. There I am a river of paintings and images. It is not frightening to me to surrender myself to my creativity, unless it is on the procreative level...

On the earth plane I am often afraid of not having "enough." Enough what? A home. Groceries. Health insurance. A piece of paper that says I have a right to live and to be happy. Something like the papers that would be given to a freed slave. When I get caught up in negative thinking I fail to notice the richness of my life today. In the last years my values have changed drastically. They have been cosmically altered for me. I've become rich on the inside. I have become insatiable for the inner wealth although I like the outer brand as well!

My art, my freedom, these have become the most important commodities in my life. They have become something to fight for, for myself and for others.

Now I have time and the context in which to do it all, be it all. Now there is room for the parts of myself that used to get forgotten on the back burners; parts which would eventually boil over, start a fire, burn down the house, destroy the neighborhood, blow up the world. It blew up my life with Philippe.

A picture of almost two years ago comes to me. In another part of my life, I work as a counselor with women who have been alcoholics and drug addicts. I like to take them out dancing sober when they are ready for it. It is a ceremony for us all, very freeing/frightening for them. It's our puberty rite. I take them to the weirdest dance place I have ever been to. They re-learn how to dance, without any rocket fuel. It is a place to dance free-form, from the gut, from the heart, from the spirit. It's full of people who just need to dance, to move to the music. We dance barefoot in everything from gowns to flowing rags and g-strings. All around is the sound of bare feet slap, slap.

Dancers move alone or in groups to every kind of music you can imagine. It is very dark. There's no smoking, no alcohol. We dance on the ceiling. We dance on the walls. We fly through the second story window, loop the loop, and fly back in again. We are Zulu warriors or we howl like wolves. If someone comes up to me I don't want to get in my face, I scream and stomp my feet — Get away! Get away! You're too close! It's heaven.

Two Halloweens back, in 1984 I attended Dance Home dressed as The Night Sky. My costume was a slithery black peignoir over leotard and tights. On my head I sculpted yards and yards of black netting. I sewed silver stars all over the black net. It was a tribute with rhinestones and glitter to the night. Halloween is Satyricon at Dance.

As I was whirling madly through the room, I caught a glimpse of myself in the walls of mirrors. I was someone else! I had joined the circus, somewhere along the line. There was a moment of illumination when the words came- "So this is what it's like to live the life of an artist." I knew I could never have been there spinning out amongst the moon and stars if I had stayed in my marriage. While it was good it was very, very good. Then it became a cage. The circus life was better for me.

WARRIOR WOMAN

I missed my husband just the same.

But it was a moment of understanding that we are sometimes granted, a bit of light against a darkening sea of self doubts. Why did I have to do it? Why did I go? Why did the voices start, forcing me to run, run, run until I knew I would go crazy unless I gave in... the voices, if ignored, would have turned me into a whore in a mansion, left behind by my Self.

This brings me back to today. This is too much writing for a Nothing. Just for today I'm going to go back to being Nothing, maybe even a loser.

I am not an artist.

Chapter 3

EXHIBITING MY WORK

Kissing them off — the artist as a bitch . . . Painting with an audience . . .

August 8, 1986

It is the night before an exhibit, and every bit of me is tense and nasty. All the preparations have been agonized over. I have made lists and I have made lists of lists I need to make.

I am in that place where my nerves are totally strung as tight as I think they can possibly go. I cannot tolerate one single request or neediness from a friend, acquaintance or non-friend. If anyone asks me for anything — time, attention, to do the dishes — I shall go straight for his or her throat.

In other words, I am exactly the opposite of everything a woman "should" be, in terms of socially expected behavior. So I fail in Behavior once again. With me it is an old subject. Not very gracious. Totally strung out on nerves. A bitch.

There is a shifting of the gears that is necessary to put together an exhibit. It's something I've had to learn or I would never get any art done, let alone put together a show. For the time it takes to get all the work done, the framing, the mailing, everything else has to be put on hold. In order to be an artist, I've had to give myself permission to do whatever it takes to get the paintings done and the show up.

I unplug my phone and turn off the answering machine. I make no attempt to return phone calls. Sometimes my life has to be treated as more important than anything else in the world. Which it really always is — Boy! It makes people mad!

There is something about people around an artist that starts this steady build of hysteria/interference at the very time when the artist needs to put every bit of heart, soul, and energy into their creative work. People sense the shift in priorities and suddenly decide they need to have the discussion they've been putting off for the last five years about what a self-centered bitch you are. They need to know you still care. I mean, you practically have to be in a hospital bed to justify taking care of yourself.

When I start a strong creative cycle or prepare for a show, I feel just a little guilty and a lot angry as I sidestep attempts to be waylaid in my focus. People need to tell you about their dreary relationships as you're dragging your displays down two flights of stairs. At least I know enough to tell them to pick up the other end of the canvas. But something has to shift to get the work done, the exhibit up. The innate, perhaps thinly disguised selfishness of the artist has to come out like a billboard in flames. "Leave me alone. I can't talk now. I'll call you in three weeks, but I think I'm going to forget. Quit pulling on me." You have to do this, if you want to get anything done. The creative side has to be treated every bit as seriously as a "straight job." It is very difficult to communicate the extreme urgency and weird timing of creativity to the people in our lives that are living by more conventional timetables. We have to work *now*, when the stuff comes gooshing up. Not from nine to five. More like from midnight on September 16 to breakfast time after the next full moon. "I won't be able to attend your wedding, the dinner party, the tupperware party, my wake. I'm painting a still-life with a frozen mongoose and I have to work fast before he defrosts between sessions. Otherwise the stink is something awful." We have to step over the bodies that litter the landscape. Not everybody is capable of understanding this. Ignore them, let them go, leave them and go paint. Abandon them if you must, but not yourself. They can call someone else or turn on a nice soap opera... Lots of people don't like artists. There are others who collect us.

Artists must get used to the slings and arrows: we are selfish. We have to become more selfish if we are to do our work. Hopefully our selfishness can be channeled, used to bring some good into the world.

The story on this grand exhibit about which I have such lofty things to say is that it is an outdoor art show. I have always stuck my nose up at outdoor shows. It is an interesting story how I came to be involved in this particular exhibit, which I participate in every year, whether I want to or not.

A friend of mine who is also an artist came to me and said she would love to be in the Santa Monica show but she was too scared. She wouldn't mind being in it if maybe I would go too. This sounded like a particularly stinking idea to me, which I told her.

The truth was I had been searching high and low for a gallery to show my work. Everywhere I went I was turned down with little politeness or interest. Galleries are generally a dead end street for me. This was the only door that had opened down a very long, very disappointing corridor, so I finally signed up. When the time came to be in the show, I asked my friend where her space was located. She told me she had never made an application. I was going to the show by myself. Thus the forces of the universe conspired to put me in my place.

The show that I had snorted at turned out to be a wonderful experience for me. I couldn't believe how much fun I had, how relaxed the atmosphere was. Someone came up to me and said, "Aren't you the one who won all the prizes?" "Huh?" I said, astutely. I didn't know it was a competition. I won a first place and two third places. Nothing could have shocked me more. There were cash awards, too, and was I hurting for some cash during my jolly divorce. I had been trying to get into galleries for a long time. I relentlessly followed every lead that was given to me, thinking maybe this time would be the big breakthrough I had worked so hard to reach, but everywhere I looked another door was slamming in my face. Here was a place where not only was I accepted, but they gave me ribbons and green stuff. I made a few sales, and I've been hooked on this show ever since.

Artistic arrogance. Get rid of it.

August 12, 1986

It has taken a day to recover from the effort of the art show. I wanted to write earlier, but I opted to do nothing, to be a blob. It's important to goof off after a show.

The show went well in the bass-ackward way they usually do. I sold a few smaller pieces there, but attracted a great deal of attention for my work. I took third prize for one of my giant flowers, the "Bird of Paradise." There is a new student starting today as the result of the show, and probably some who will start later as a result. I got some newspaper publicity.

It is very, very hard to live with exhibits but no sales. It embarrasses me when people ask if I sold much. Somehow it feels as if something must be wrong with me, with the way I do the show, that I am not pushy enough. Everyone has some inane suggestion about what to do to sell, and it makes me crazy. I want to flee, but I am gracious. "You were showing *flowers* ?" she will say as if I had been mooning the crowds. "No wonder you didn't sell any." This from a woman who didn't see the show. "Flowers are the only thing people buy," I shrieked. I was not gracious that time, or thankful for her helpful suggestions. "You price them too low — too high — too in the middle. You should pay people to take them." Everyone knows just how an artist should go about selling her work.

How can I keep a good attitude if I am not an immediate success? How can I keep dragging myself back to the sometimes ungratifying exhibits? I have to look at the big picture. Some pieces are sold before and after the exhibit itself. This is what keeps me doing shows. If I don't exhibit I can have a warehouse full of beautiful paintings that no one will ever see. I have to exhibit, even if I don't like it or it is discouraging, or it terrifies me, which it does most of the time.

The most important thing is that the compulsion to create still comes pushing out, along with the paintings. I think perhaps I will take a break now from the more commercial side of my work and produce some of the larger pieces. Sphinxes slither through my dreams and haunt my hallways. The Emperor awaits. They send me messages — "Come, come paint us. Leave the rest behind." Why not? I plan on working on them out by the garbage cans next

23

to the garage, because there is no longer any room to bring them in or hang them. I will paint right in the storage area. Simple.

One of the things I do which I love during these exhibits is paint on the site. I pick a nice place under a tree, so I can use its energy. I find a place where there is not too much sun filtering through the trees, which is incredibly draining. I put on a hat, take off my shoes and get down to what I do best. This has taken care of the crisis of having to be charming for too many hours in a row. I don't have to talk to people in those incredibly strained and phoney conversations we are expected to get into at exhibits. I just do what I love doing, and it turns out that's the best thing I could possibly do.

I have a great French paint box that folds out into an easel and a tabouret. I hang up my wind chimes and a brightly painted Japanese cloth fish in the tree so I feel like I'm in my own studio — which of course I really am. I usually buy some brilliant flowers. I favor pink, violet and purple petunias for the job, but dead fish and leeks would do just as well. All this arty action and color attracts a great deal of interest from the crowd.

The best part of these exhibits is when I start to paint. Suddenly there will be a crowd of twenty or thirty people in back of me. At times they want to get quite close, like right at my sides. They are mesmerized by the great conjuring act of the Artist At Work. Artists turn Nothing into Something. We make garbage into sculpture. We turn blobs of gooey paint into images ripped right out of the unconscious of man and womankind.

Sometimes someone will very slowly reach out a hand and gingerly touch a tube of paint, fearing perhaps that I will slap their hand. But their actions at this time are as fascinating to me as mine are to them. How reverentially they observe. How lovely to feel the tribe there with me while I paint, participating in their own ways. For a few hours I am not a lonely artist.

While I am there painting in the park, I experience some of the things I like best about human beings. Their childlike curiosity and desire to talk comes through, even when they aren't using words. They are full of wonder, respect, the desire to learn, the need to create. They want to help — to squeeze my paint tubes for me or get me a nice rag. This is the human race at their best... they are as full of awe as undestroyed children. They are silent, and ready for something indefinable — something a little magical. They are actively assisting the artistic process by their interest and attentiveness. The people love art. They would like to be closer to it.

The first time I tried painting at a show, it was purely because I didn't know what else to do. I didn't know how to talk to people, or to disengage from people that I didn't like. As I turned to get a tube of paint from my chair, I nearly jumped out of my skin. There was a crowd of perhaps twenty-five people. This was a horrible shock to a people-hater. Sweat rolled down my inner arms, into my palms and off the end of my finger tips. I could hear comments spoken softly, wondering what kind of paint it was, about my bare feet or my hair. After my initial shock and self-consciousness, I was touched by the beauty of the experience. The sunlight was perfect and the wind was flying through my hair. The park was on a cliff above the ocean. The smell of the sea was all-pervasive. I could feel the love that people have for the artists. I may not always show a profit, but I profit greatly from the love.

Chapter 4

THE SPHINX RISES

Tarot series . . . I can't stop writing . . . Divorce trauma . . . Art Speak

August 14, 1986

Two days ago I started work on two enormous paintings — the two I was waiting to work on until I had more space. They pushed themselves out without waiting for my permission. Sometimes I feel like a pregnant woman who is walking down the street, her water breaking as she walks, twins, triplets, quadruplets squirting out of her as she tries to maintain the illusion that nothing out of the ordinary is going on. I walk along the city streets bustling with everyday life, sometimes squatting in the crowd. Painted things keep flying out of me without my control. It feels a little like I should be holding my skirts down.

The first painting is the 5' x 7' of a sphinx in the middle of the desert. There are three pyramids in the distance. There are also some pyramid seedlings emerging from the sand. Copper-colored snakes stream along beside her in the sand. All are in sinuous motion. The sands are shifting. The Sphynx is preparing to move too — her wings are lifted and she is shedding her old skin as she prepares for flight. The new moon and the sun are in the ambiguous sky.

The second painting is the fifth in my series of the major arcana in the Tarot. The Emperor is taking form in my living room, next to the Empress. She is waiting for him in the woods. He is seated with a beautiful lion, the lion of strength. The lion aids him in his developing wisdom. There is a tree in the background with a Shadow-Man with the head of a ram. The Shadow-Man is his ally. The Emperor holds a crude wooden staff to symbolize his sovereignty, and there is a small golden torch burning at the top of his staff illuminating his place in the forest. This image is very, very hard for me to work with. The Emperor reminds me of my father.

I have been working on these two and studying them. I have trained myself to gaze at them, into them, without opinion, judgement or criticism. That is how I learn about my paintings and their structure. I look, and I look, and I look.

If the artist can really train herself to *see* , she doesn't need the criticism of others to find the strengths and weaknesses of her work. It sounds so simple, and yet it is perhaps the last secret revealed to the artist. One needs to develop the faculty of artistic intuition. This is the thing you cannot get a crash course in. It takes years to clear the pathways. This is something not everyone can learn. Some teachers can help with this, but most can't. I don't think there is anything wrong with studying art one's entire life. When I studied with one of my favorite teachers, Sueo Serisawa, there came a time when he said, "You have gotten the technique of painting down. Now we need to develop the quality of intuition." He was a master of this. Sueo was a very intuitively evolved man.

We would set the painting down at the far end of the room and just look at it for perhaps fifteen or twenty minutes. We would ignore it. We would drink tea. He would stick little torn up pieces of paper to the wet canvas to find the bit of color that would solve our dilemma. We would turn it upside down and inside out. How fortunate I was to have him as my teacher. When the time came for him to move on I wept for days. I felt lost.

It's surprising how much of what he taught me is still in there. I still call on his teachings every time I paint. It is all still alive and fresh. I think, in fact, that I will write to him. The past has been tugging at me terribly the last few days. More unfinished business.

Same Day, Later On

I had a most revealing day, at least in terms of my inner journey. I had an appointment with my therapist, Don Dubin. All artists should have their head examined. We are a challenge for the therapists of the world. ("And you *imagined* a three-headed dog in your bed, you mean." "No. I *saw* him. He lives there with the flamingos.") We talked about many things, and as I described to him the "Nothing," my voice began to get louder and louder. I began throwing a lot of expletives into my language. I realized that I was furious about a lot of trash and injustice in my life. I was thoroughly on fire. It seemed so clear suddenly that sometimes the "Nothing" is frozen rage. Not always. Nothing is always. But the anger is a pathway out. Or in.

Years ago I made a commitment to feel all of my feelings, no matter what. I knew I needed to do it to heal emotionally. Sometimes that seems to require a lot of detective work, much excavation. Certainly it brings a shitload of pain. If I don't do my emotional maintenance, I can coldly watch the creative torrent slow to a trickle and then dry up. The commitment to feel is a commitment to live. It's also a major commitment to my creativity.

When I left Don I was overcome by the desire to see my first art teacher, Dorothy Royer. Her house was close to his office. I have wanted to stop by her house for many years — ten years, in fact. I always came up with some reason why I couldn't. She might be busy, she might not remember me. Today I parked my truck under a tree and knocked at the door unannounced. "It's Tina!"

Her face was radiant, as usual. Her face was a beacon of light in an often frightening world. It was this radiance from within that attracted me back to her after thirteen years. Dorothy was my art teacher when I was five years old. I returned to her a confused, suicidal 18-year-old. My feelings after seeing her today are like a daughter seeing the wise and loving woman who raised her after a long, long absence.

She taught me to paint and play with art when I was a little girl. She told me not to use an eraser. If I made a mistake I was to try to use it in my picture in some way. One day when I was painting a rose, she came to me and said, "It looks like you've been painting the same tired old rose the same exact way all your life (all five years). Why don't you try to do something different." I never forgot her instructions. I still rarely use an eraser! I doubt the existence of mistakes. She found a way to give me guidelines in art, as did Dorothy Cannon, without crushing my spontaneity.

On today's visit I went through the old studio where we used to paint. I recognized a Japanese bowl I used to swish my water color brushes in. That was at the time of my return to her at age eighteen. I worked with her for several years then, and she passed on her teachings on the subject of art therapy. I thought of going to school to get a certificate in the school system, but I didn't think I would ever find such a wise teacher. The school system didn't offer the same intimate contact that I was getting, or the hands-on training Dorothy gave so generously. She was one of the best, and I knew it.

She recommended me for a job working with the probation department. I was teaching the probation officers how to do art therapy, and working with the kids as well. At that time I was probably having the worst hangovers of my drinking career. I suffered from monstrous headaches and shaking. The probation officers must have hated this 20-year-old coming in and telling them what to do.

A tremendous amount of pain came from that learning experience, between the p.o.'s rather limited ability to grasp the principals of creativity, and my headaches. The kids themselves terrified me. There were guards and barbed wire everywhere. Not enough to suit me. So much for a career in art therapy...

I need some time to digest my visit to Dorothy. When I am about to make gigantic changes, I find I desperately need to make pilgrimages to all my old temples. I want to talk to my old teachers and friends. There is something of the vision quest about the process.

August 20, 1986

The moon was full and disturbing last night. I couldn't sleep so rather than fight it I decided to get up and work.

I am reading Henry Miller's *Tropic of Capricorn* at the moment. I love his books. I especially love what he writes about art. He's one of the few people who writes about painting in a way that's not full of bullshit. I guess that's because he was a painter himself. I loved his paintings the first time I saw them. As I was exposed to the "World of Art" I grew to love their genuine quality even more. I realized how few artists were willing or able to work in this child-like way. Pure painting.

When I was broke, living in the chicken coop, I used to read the lives of various artists, seeking out those who had had a very difficult time of it. Their stories gave me hope. I loved to read Henry Miller when I was running on empty. He was so broke, broke, broke — but he lived the life of an artist. Somehow it took the insult out of my discouraging existence. I was terrified of not having enough money. When money came, it came out of nowhere. Money Comes to Destitute Artist From the Great Void. Miller's life was hard-edged, as mine was at that time. As I read his work, I saw myself in there, looking for my path. I wasn't just a screw-up. I was an artist.

In the library of the chicken coop I also read Georgia O'Keefe's autobiography. I was particularly interested in the parts about her much older husband and mentor, Stieglitz. I clutched the book to me as I read about her separation from him, of her need to get away from him, the family, their life, the world. I grasped at it like a person gone over a cliff clutching at twigs, hoping this was "What Was Wrong With Me." Everyone seemed to have an opinion on that subject.

What a horror story that part of my life was. It still gives me the creeps as I remember the sharks circling around me. All around me I could see people who once seemed to care about me revelling in my fall from the Enchanted Life, my fall from glory, my crash into the gutter, to become just another piece of human detritus, going to my just desserts — the constrictions of a job, an ordinary life, financial insecurity.

The time of my divorce was my Trial by Fire. I believe all of us who are called to an alternative path must be subjected to this painful burning away that serves to clear out the faint-hearted, the dilettantes, the insincere. It also weeds out the so-called friends. Too bad it doesn't weed out the assholes, but they too seem to be strengthened by the process.

Each time we are passed through the fire we become stronger and stronger, like a blade of steel. It is an essential process to give us the strength to be different from the 99 1/2 %, as Serisawa used to say. We have a way of bringing it upon ourselves, this necessary testing. It is a gift — a beautiful, burning gift for which one is grateful. It is the pain in my life that has made me different from the other little boys and girls. The pain has forced me to grow.

When I didn't have the desire to live anymore for myself, I would remember my art and my cat. Well, I'll stick around to feed the cat. Then I'll paint a picture about how fucked all of this is, about how much I hate everyone, about how ugly people look to me under fluorescent lights, about how distorted their faces seem. I'll paint myself crying. Always crying. La Llorona. It is the pain that has given me the need to create as if my life depended on it. And my life *has* depended on it.

August 22, 1986

I can't stop working. Everything is an intrusion, an irritation. I don't even want to stop working to eat. It's this damned writing. It's like having a boss who won't let you leave the office — "Just one more thing, Le Marque," ...or... "Look at this! You've got to come look at this! Don't leave! You haven't heard the one about the..." And so on. I can't eat and I can't sleep. I'm exhausted and exhilarated. Why it's almost like being in love.

If I surrender to the insatiable beast I know it will chew me up and shit me out, boneless, without eyes, fingers rubbed off right up to the knuckles. I will fall out of the asshole of the creature at the end of my life, everything spent, with me a dried-up, old hag.

This is the meaning of art to me, on certain days when I haven't slept for too many nights in a row. I am crabby, not right in the head. Sure, sure. I'd rather go work in a bank. I'd fit right in there... under the desk or something. Maybe a nice, tight, safety deposit box.

I went to see Schifrin today. It must be the season of pilgrimages. I am making little visits to all my past icons, carefully laying sage and mangoes upon their altars. Please, please, can't you take me back into the playpen which I fell out of, into the shark-pool?

Schifrin. He is like the Shakespearean actor's interpretation of an artist. The ego of a lion and the heart and personality to match. From the first time I went to his studio, when he lived up in Topanga, I wanted him to love me, to think of me as his darling student. Why?

I always went to interview the artists I studied with, to make sure they were not big jerks or perhaps lousy painters, because one finds this rather often in teaching situations. I always ask to see their work. That has been one of my objections to art school. I have no idea how or if this fat-head professor who is telling me what to do, grading me, critiquing me, trying to influence me, paints himself. One should be sure. Don't go to a plastic surgeon whose wife looks as if she has been hit in the face with a shovel.

Thusly I found myself in the studio of Arnold Schifrin. He was there, in all his glory. The Artist in his Castle. I learned later that his life had just been utterly torn up by tragedy, but like the great actor that he was, he went on with the show. He was welcoming. He liked the painting of a cityscape that I brought to show him. I loved his strange work which reminded me of Cuevas, a favorite artist. He loved the red bandana I wore around my head. When he told me I could come paint at his studio, I felt as if I had been admitted to a world not available to everyone, into the Royal Order of Artists.

I studied with him for about five years, I think. He was an excellent teacher for me, always respecting my way of working. He never made an extraneous comment about my work, but filled the studio with many interesting stories. There were some terrific painters there. The studio overflowed with laughter.

It was the kind of studio where I loved to work. Every topic is discussed: art, film, radio, food (Of course! Every studio has this in common!), how to do everything you ever heard of, bail-bondsmen, drugs, sex, and particularly, taboo subjects.

As the years go by I know more and more how lucky I was to find the teachers I studied with. They opened up many aspects of the world to me that I could only see corners of before. They taught me what the beast was, where to hunt it down and what weapons to use. I loved the work I did while studying with Arnold. Perhaps if I could get away from this god-damned computer I could go paint with him once in awhile. I am just as hungry as ever to learn. I just don't have any free time anymore — I'm writing.

From time to time I still think I should go to a regular art school. But it feels to me like I've come to a closure of my student days. I mean, I'm always learning, it's just that finally you realize you've pulled out in front of the pack. You can't double back on your tracks and pretend you aren't where you are. I think sometimes it would be great to go to an art school now and get a degree. I don't think I am going to get the time anymore. It feels like now it is a time of accomplishment and attainment. I just took a different route up the mountain.

Later that same day...

I've lost all concept of time. I know that this is later, or later that *same* day. I see that it is daylight. It seems important at some time during each day to acknowledge *some* reality, if only as a jumping off place. Clock-time is a landmark to which I can occasionally point and say, "I've been here before. I think I should eat breakfast." Or, "It's 4:15 in the morning. I used to sleep at this time, didn't I?"

To continue, I spent a lot of time today mulling over my visit with Schifrin. "I thought that you were doing so well with your husband. You were developing so beautifully. After that, I didn't understand."

Does anyone think I understand? Leaving a perfectly good and definitely exciting marriage to be with a dog trainer? If I had been sixteen and run off with a circus performer and his trained ape, I couldn't have elicited more shock and disapproval. It was about the same, really.

First, I shot myself out of a cannon. That's not easy! Then out came the tigers and the high-wire. There were the obligatory hoops of fire to be jumped through, again and again. Here, to top it off I'll put my head in the lion's mouth. That should put out my burning hair.

All the time we are talking in the sunset-washed alley in back of the studio I can see my too-vivid reflection in the rear window of my truck. My face is showing plenty of creases on the forehead. I look like hell to myself as I am standing there, jabbering. Schifrin is a seer. I see him seeing this, too. I am nervous, smiling overmuch. I look down to see if I have my pants on. I am moving too fast to put on an act. I look shaken. Today I ran faster and faster, away from the past.

Re: my divorce — which I am sick of explaining, some friends said, "You were a bird in a gilded cage." Screw you. Others tell me how bad he was for me, how he dominated me, how my work has been rocketed into another dimension since I left. Only a few of the old souls knew the truth. I loved him, turning myself inside out. That is why I had to steal back my power. A few understand. I have grown since I left — "exploded" is a better word.

Today I am mad. I have painted and written and taught all day long. I have succeeded in living under my own terms, in ways it cannot be done. I don't subscribe to "The Real World." I don't have a local address. I haven't left this world exactly, but entered a parallel plane.

Every sight, every note of music that I hear, starts a torrent of pictures, words, memories: I miss you. Can you finally hear me now? I anxiously await our inevitable meeting in the next experience. We can't get along in this one.

August 25, 1986

It is 6:30 a.m. and I am awake and wide-eyed. If I am awake because I am driven to work, I say I am wired. If I am just awake, staring at the ceiling, I then say I am weird. I am tired and wired. At any rate, I don't usually wake up early unless my fleabag of a cat wakes me up.

She has a cruel method of doing this. She likes to wait until I am deeply and blissfully asleep. She then takes a flying start from across the living room. She plans all of this mathematically, fiendishly, to land hard on all fours right in the middle of my stomach. "An Ode to a Cat"-that is how I happen to be awake working at this unnatural hour. It is the work of a demon from the pound.

Last night I went to the birthday party of a friend. Something happened there which was new to me — I could talk! Usually I am extremely anxious going into any social situation, especially parties and exhibits. I become so nervous that sweat uncontrollably pours off of me, sometimes rolling down the entire length of my arm and delicately dropping off from my rigid fingertips. I hate it. I cannot think of why I came, and I hate everyone at the party. I can't leave soon enough. I have left many a social gathering through the back door. People who know me don't take it personally. I just can't stand groups of people.

The thing that was different about last night was that someone asked me about my work. With all of the writing I am doing, I have become pretty adept at verbalizing what I'm doing. In fact I couldn't shut up. For the first time that I can recall, I was comfortable in this social get-together. I didn't feel out of place or like a lump with nothing to say. I could talk about my paintings and about everything else I was doing with my art.

It opened up a world that has always remained just out of my grasp. It has been really helpful, the writing and the teaching both, in learning to articulate about what it is that I do. It's become an area that I can communicate about. In fact it's a pleasure.

I have always shunned people who spoke about their art as bullshitters. Better to be in the studio doing it. I have learned over the years not to speak about my projects before they were well underway, if at all, as it lessened the urgent need to actually roll up one's sleeves and force it, create it, do it. It was as if in the telling, the need to communicate was already filled. I didn't want to extinguish even a little of the fire. It is one of the drives I harness to pull my idea out of the muck and get it on the canvas.

However, the only way to get people over to the studio to see the work and enjoy it, is to let them know that I'm an artist. My skills in sales, verbal communication, public relations in fact, have been largely undeveloped until very recently.

I used to make a point to attend several gallery openings before I would have my own exhibit. I would get something to drink and station myself next to some very chatty group. During the time that I was pretending to look at the paintings on the wall, I was secretly learning the language. I was, after all, a Martian dropped to earth in a human's body, adroitly mimicking the people and the sounds that they made, all senseless to me, of course. *What the hell are they talking about???* After as much of this as I could stand, I would tear out into the night, bored and ill at ease. I could sound like an artist for several days after that. I was just as full of shit as anyone, and the stress of it all used to bring on incredible headaches. Perhaps my mask was on a little tight? Smile cranked up one notch too many?

Anyway, last night I was able to blabber away like a real fountain of artisisms. It felt wonderful. It wasn't fake — I had just developed a new skill. I have finally found something I can contribute to a gathering, other than endless self-deprecating remarks about how neurotic I am or how much I hate people and/or parties. When I had nothing left to say, I shut up. I wasn't a wallflower and I wasn't a phoney.

Shitballs! There is a common fear voiced by people who are stalling their creativity. They feel that there is a painting, maybe a poem, that they would really like to try to do. They follow this by saying that if they do this one piece, that'll be the end of it. They won't have anything else to say or do after that. Or they lack the skills to do it well enough.

So what? Do it anyway, then become a nobody with one painting done from the heart. Beats going to the grave never having taken the chance. There are voices inside of me that whisper the same poisonous messages, but the truth is the more I work, the more work pours out of me. The only slowing there has ever been in this deluge has been when I stopped for a moment to think. A month later they were still trying to get my head out of my ass.

Over the years I have learned not to think. Do you think you need to think? That is your head jacking itself off, telling you and everyone else how supreme, how delectable, how indispensable it is, how essential to life, to your very survival. Me, I get in trouble every time I think, like when I was first learning to drive a stick shift. Every time I made a move I had to think. I have never moved in so disjointed and ineffectual a way. What do I do instead of thinking? I jump. I drop down into the chasm. I do not think unless there is no other alternative. I watch. I do it. I surrender. I come to the cliff and I jump, again and again.

Now about friends — or the people in my life. All my life I have been blessed with very close, long-term friendships. In the last few months I have lost three of my closest friends. Also there was my divorce and the ensuing exodus. I saw it coming, and there was nothing I could do to prevent it other than prostitute myself. The sad thing was that the breaches all came over the same issue. I said no. No, I can't do this. No, I can't go there. That's all it took for them to take up the offensive. Then, to my surprise I saw myself take out my machete, heard myself telling them to go screw themselves.

Two of these were very intimate friendships that had been in my life for over eleven years. What was really strange was the reaction I had to the losses. Rather than curl up in pain, I set off down the road without a single regret. With each removal I found myself feeling freer, more pulled to paint, more centered. Somehow these relationships which had at one time had given me so much strength and support had become invisible mooring lines, imperceptibly tying me down. Their expectations were subtly holding me "in place." For me, when you can't say no, the friendship is over.

Once these strangling little connections were cut, my own strength automatically kicked in. I thought I was weak and would crumble, but I did not. The idea of channeling myself into my work when I was under siege really never occurred to me before. There was a void that began to fill itself with art.

Chapter 5

WOMAN ON FIRE
Cambria, California, and points south . . .

September 5, 1986

I have been away from my work for over a week. It has been a productive week, just the same. I moved my parents into their new home in Cambria. I worked on a portrait, or the closest thing I come to a portrait, of my friend, Jeanne. It is a painting *about* her, more than a traditional portrait.

She is very happy with it. I am happy, too. Sometime during the course of it I invited her back to have a look. "Oh! You need more terra cotta." "Shut up, Jeanne." Every twenty years or so I indulge myself and give someone I owe my life to a painting. There is a special freedom to an unpaid commission.

Since I returned from my trip to Cambria I have been out of my mind, feeling the empty mouths of the world pulling at me. The first rule of healing is to be healed . I need time to listen to myself, to know if I need to take rather than to give. Everything from my childhood wants to divert my energy and take care of everyone else. My nature is to try fill their needs, even when I have nothing left to give. What I did was tell my friends that I was going out of my mind with the strain of trying to carry the weight of the world on my back. I can't afford to go out of balance anymore. I used to be able to really indulge in emotional tangents and rescue binges of every description. Since I have made a deeper commitment to myself and my art, I must come before the other empty mouths. I become enraged if I don't place myself first. If I get angry and don't let it out, the creative circuitry goes dead when the anger goes underground.

I have spent most of my life trying to prove it is okay for me to be alive, to be happy. I must have paid the debt, because now I want to live and to work, no excuses for my presence in the world, no apologies. Would-be friends fly away, totally furious whenever I dare to say "no." I find the word "no" to be a natural house cleaner! It automatically makes time to work.

If you think you don't have any time to write, paint, dance, fly, "just say no" to a few friends. It will free up months for you.

This weekend I'm going to speak at a convention in Palm Springs. I'm going to take my book to record my sneaking dark little thoughts as they try to scuttle away into the shadows. I don't know anyone where I am going, but for the last three months I have been dreaming steadily about one of the other speakers, Bob Earll. I don't know why. I keep dreaming that I'm supposed to go talk to him... I wouldn't know him if I bumped into him. It all seems a big adventure.

September 10, 1986

I visited my teacher, Arnold Schifrin again. I noticed he was wearing a dress. He has awful legs. He shouldn't wear dresses. We were trying to have a conversation when suddenly I could not control myself any longer. Why the hell are you wearing a dress? He told me it was a political thing, too long and boring to explain. That's about what I think of politics, I thought to myself.

I found him rummaging through a bag of sacred stones in my purse. There was much clicking as he rattled them too roughly. I made an angry gesture to tell him to treat them reverently. He was putting some in his pocket, the sneaking coyote! I reached into his pocket while he was laughing. It was full of crystals, rose quartz, Apache tears. I cannot trust you! He laughed. I teased him more about his awful legs and made ready to leave.

Sneaking into his kitchen, I found a potato masher full of chromium oxide green paint. After several attempts to get just the right amount of paint on a brush, I find the right spot on the light switch. I made my secret mark on his wall.

Arnold in his usual bizarre behavior mode was pulling on his shawl. I told him I have known two other men who wore skirts, and that it really did not upset me except that his scrawny little bird legs were so ugly to look at.

We left, realizing we were on a bus and that we might miss our stop. As I left the doorway I found myself at the front of a huge doorway alone. There was no stairway down and out, only the steepest building front to be scaled with fingernails bleeding. With extreme anxiety, I began the steep descent because I am always willing to do whatever has to be done.

Where before there had been nothing visible to my fearful and limited focus, some people on a stairway materialized to my right. They were calling to me. "You don't have to go down the hard way!." I scrambled back up and awaited their arrival. We sat together. Suddenly there was no pressure. An easy descent was now clearly visible to take when the time was right.

With great relief on my part, we sat and relaxed together. It was a very nice man and his daughter. They had three little shaggy black poodle pups with them. They were the most beautiful and loving pups I had seen. I wanted to get one for my mother, as a gift.

When I began to play with the special one, they told me her name was La Encanta, the Enchanted One. I realized then that I was walking in the dreamtime. I decided to return to Arnold to tell him this. One of me returned to him to explain that I had had this experience with him in the dream state. The other aspect of me felt no need to ever return. I remained to love La Encanta. I wanted nothing but to be with her, my little spirit animal.

I am working on the "Sphinx in the Sea of Snakes." My life is saturated with the supernatural. Weird things are happening all around me. I am in my element. I am drinking from hidden deep wells of the spirit and I feel complete.

I would be leaving out the thoughts foremost in my mind if I did not mention that I had one of the most extraordinary meetings of my extremely adventurous life this weekend. The gods of the desert had lured me there for a rendezvous with a writer, visionary and madman, Bob Earll. I was called, and I followed the call alone and unarmed. There followed a meeting of the spirits which I had dreamt of, but only for others, people in books.

I was compelled from within to go on this trip and it has altered the direction of my life completely. Something sacred happened to me and I want to hold it close to my heart.

In Palm Springs I found myself under the desert stars, listening to their chatter. The stars crackled with energy. I burst into flames and for three days I could not stop burning. The hot desert wind was blowing, whipping me into a more spectacular conflagration. I was a woman on fire. The desert was densely black that night and I could be seen glowing for miles.

When the wind blew it wrapped a spell around me with this man's assistance, covering me with sand so very, very slowly that I did not know what was happening until it was too late. I found myself buried, unable to climb out of the pyramid. The sand was filled with lizards and snakes that brushed up against me. I could no longer resist. By the time I realized what was happening, the sand was just under my wide-open eyes. My world was ablaze with spirit lightning.

Suddenly I was ripped from the sand, torn from my mother. Rootless, I was a tumbleweed blowing wildly down the great wide-open.

I left me behind, goodbye. Another person came back to Los Angeles. I am smouldering still, unable to cool. When people touch me they pull their hands back in surprise. "My God! You are hot! Are you sick? What are you doing?"— believe me, I don't know. Something's happening, though—something big. I look in the mirror and I see the face of a ghost. My friends are worried about me, I know, but they needn't be. It is too late for that because whoever I was up until now is dead.

I wish I could go out under the desert sky and let my spirit be soothed and cooled by the stars. Here in my studio in Los Angeles I've thrown myself into frenzied painting. The more I work, the more comes pouring out. I'm on fire, and I am throwing gasoline on myself.

Each day I am dying. My whole life is passing before my eyes.

September 17, 1986

Yesterday was my 35th birthday and it was weird, to say the least. Awful, too. I went out for dinner with Kelly. He was cold and abrasive. Something doesn't fit there anymore, and I'm not sure what it is. Something just doesn't feel right. Whatever feelings Kelly had for me when he first asked me to move in with him have gotten lost. I don't feel loved by him anymore.

Parallel worlds feel more like home to me at this time. In the dreamworld I was walking down the street with a tiny baby in my arms. Chile Bean came dashing out aggressively from in back of me. I was worried about what it was that she saw. In the every day world I must always contain her, control her, hold her on a tight leash in this place of spiritual confinement. It makes me sick and angry to do it, and yet I am obligated to not let the wolfish spirit of my beautiful dog free on the grey streets of Los Angeles. She might attack a dead person or a rapist or something.

I was preoccupied with details of my impending painting trip to Joshua Tree when I remembered that I had a tiny baby in my arms, me, of all people! I felt that she was cold, and I pulled her very close to me to warm us both. I wondered what she was doing in my arms, this sweet dark-eyed baby. With a start I realized that Chile had slipped the leash, passed outside the confines of my consciousness.

Suddenly I was painfully hungry. I would starve unless I ate immediately. I saw a rack of cookies where there were none before. I didn't particularly want a cookie, but I forced myself to chew one and swallow it. I was worried about Chile, that she might become wild on me, biting people she didn't like, chasing down neurotic little city squirrels. I felt so hemmed in, all that kept me going was knowing I would be at the Oasis of Mara within less than 24 hours. My being would be recharged there, all the broken pieces gluing themselves back together with the energy of the desert doing the healing for me.

BANG! The sound of a gunshot shocked me out of my image stream. I jumped up in alarm before realizing it was the sound of an art book hitting the bare floor. It was the book I have been consumed with, *The Art of New Mexico, Paths to Taos and Santa Fe* hitting the wood as hard as a rock. I felt as if I had been hit on the head by my dream, as well as the book. Although I realized I had been dreaming, the dream continued uninterrupted. I felt that the book *was* hitting me on the head, along with the dream.

WARRIOR WOMAN

The pull of Santa Fe is dragging me by the feet, enchanting me. I sense that my future is there, pulling me towards it. As I lay in the dark, wired for sound, I feel the suck of the desert on my soul. I argue with myself that I cannot do this, I don't know how, I haven't a cent, I will not place myself in a position where I must interrupt the urgent flow of my work. I resist, resist, but I know the path will win in the end. When we are called, the Great Spirit finds a way to cover all the costs. I'm in the grinder now. I can feel myself being eaten alive. I'm in the ripping process of surrender to the waves of change.

It is impossible for any of this to happen. I want this to go on record, so that I can watch from the grandstand and see how it is all brought about. The desert is pulling me back, like the Great Mother, pulling back her child who is lost and crying. Me—the baby in my dreams. At least in my dream I am in my own arms—a good sign.

The moon is full and I cannot sleep. I am so exhausted I could drop and yet the compulsion to work and the momentum of the dream fill me with the energy I can only give in to. Just wake up and work.

Something else happened on my birthday. I went into the bathroom. Looking up unexpectedly in the mirror I caught a completely unveiled view of myself. I saw a woman like a frightened deer peering at me out of tormented red eyes. She was paralyzed by pain. She was too startled to move as I let my inner vision bore into her burned out eyes.

The ravages of all my turmoil were there unmasked upon my face. I was being torn to shreds before my eyes. I was so shocked by the wreckage of my face, I ran to the garage for a canvas, hoping the vision would still be there when I returned. I had to take the chance of leaving for a canvas. I crept back into the darkening black bathroom, praying that I would not frighten this animal part of me away, frightening her off into the dark thickets never to be seen again. Approaching cautiously, I was relieved to find her there still. Her shirt was off, and she grasped a bright bit of fabric for a primitive and magical defense, the Shield of Color.

As I began to work feverishly, I could feel the distress of her soul, feel the disintegration as clearly as if it were happening to me. Compassion washed over me. I ignored it and hurried on, to capture the essence of her soul before the spell was broken and she fled. It was getting dark fast.

As I worked, her inner aspects began to reveal themselves to me on the unseen levels where I operate. The painting began to paint itself, her soul superimposing itself over my own small will. It was the soul of a primitive, the wolf unleashed. It was the Woman Who Hides! She was in full war paint, the unedited, unhomogenized color of her soul. I felt honored by her self-revelation, her courage in appearing full-faced before my eyes. She was terrified, but radiant with the madness brought on by an act of great courage. A Warrioress, she stood before me, naked and unarmed. I wept. She wept with me. It was hard to see to paint, but the painting became truer.

I saw her there shattering in the process of undoing all that needs to be undone. She was surrounded by lightening bolts, entangled with her little brother, the coral snake who appeared before her on the horse trail not too long ago. Her face, her body, her mind, her life, all ravaged... Everything that is, but her Soul.

It was a horrifying face, all veneer and nicety and illusion stripped away. She was caught off guard in the place of terror and initiation. For me they are the same. It was my moment of absolute clarity. Lines were cut. Bonds were severed. Glass was broken and all bridges burned.

This is one of the most powerful paintings I have ever done. Upon viewing her, people face their chairs in another direction or leave the room altogether. It is the face of utter human disintegration. I do not expect anyone to like it. But I have been waiting for her on this side of the rock for a lifetime. I would have waited an eternity for a single glimpse of the wild woman I needed desperately to contact. I am lucky it took so many years, because I could never have withstood the Medusian shock. She wore the mask of all I fear, and she is my initiation into my next life.

I painted her however, and now I hold a corner of her soul, just as she holds a corner of my own.

September 18, 1986

It has been so long since I have been able to sleep that I have ceased to resist. I'm going out into the desert tomorrow morning. In the mornings, in the nights, I just get up and work on this recording of my life which is calling me for reasons that are not known to me. Sometimes there is such a sense of anticipation about whatever is coming that is causing my agitation that I am awakened out of a dead sleep. I realize that even in my sleep I am preparing, for what I do not know. It is just a distant coyote call at this point, a spirit sensed but unseen far off in time or maybe arriving today. I simply cannot rest.

After drifting off to a trance-like sleep for several hours I was awakened by the Dance of the Cat-Fiend. I came up enough levels to become conscious of the information being transferred back and forth inside of me. It was as if I had come upon a primitive tribe in the deep caves of my dream state. The tribal elders were

41

instructing the less experienced of the dream travellers. It was significant enough that I want to write it here. These are the same landmarks we all find on our journey.

First, I was being given instructions as to how I should finish the painting of the Sphinx. I felt she had more to say, and so I have been looking at her, watching, listening. She is surrounded by a sea of snakes. Now she too is shedding her skin. There was a whole tribe of wise women and men. They talked to me about my paintings of the tarot cards and the information concealed in their symbolism. They talked to me about the abrupt change in direction my life was about to take.

The most important piece of information I was given was regarding fear. They told me that the reason I feel so terrible is only that I am afraid. I was directed to a breathing process. Inhale the light. Let it do the work. Exhale the darkness. Let it heal. Let it all go.

The message was that I do not have to be afraid. Everything is going to be done for me. I must take off my brakes and allow everything to happen, to crumble, to fall. The Tower. I must take my bleeding claws out of the cliff I am hanging onto.

There were other more personal messages they passed to me in the pre-dawn darkness. Those messages were for me alone, and their purpose is to raise my level to one of joyous anticipation.

I sound like a lunatic. That's all I expect to be at this time. Nevertheless, I know that the level and the personal nature of what I am revealing is going to bring me a bumper crop to of animosity. I will reap as never before from the seeds I am planting now. There is a secret motive behind all of this: it is the path to my freedom. I want to grow until I don't know myself anymore. I want to break open and the seeds to spread far and wide. I want to give it all away. I must let myself be killed off one more time so I can rise like a phoenix from the ashes. Am I crazy? Frighteningly so. Ask anyone who thinks they know me. But I am also a star of hope in the night for those who have been called out into the Unknown. It can be done.

Chapter 6

FUNERAL OF THE ARTIST AND DEATH OF A LOVER
Moving trucks . . . Exodus from the City of the Fallen Angels . . .

October 1, 1986

It has been some time since I have been able to make an entry. It was revealed to me in a most painful way that Kelly has been cheating on me royally. A few days after my birthday he failed to come home one night. I don't know about you, but that's one of the ways I would rudely notify someone that I was sleeping with someone else. I got the message immediately and unmistakably. That must have been the disturbance that I have been feeling but unable to identify. What a shock! I left myself wide open to trusting him.

Since then my life has been falling apart with such rapidity that I couldn't spare even a moment to write. My life is disintegrating and I am painting as never before. Sometimes he doesn't come home all night. I have been sleeping on the couch in the studio. I awaken at ungodly hours and paintings pour out of me like a river. So do the tears. Hour after hour I am pulled back to my canvas. I don't know where else to go. The pain is devastating. I almost do not sleep. I can't believe that this man who has been such a friend to me, who has shared my bed for four years has betrayed me. I trusted him completely.

I am working on the Sphinx painting. She is my vehicle out of here. I am rapidly trying to complete my last series of four paintings from Joshua Tree. It makes me long for the desert, but perhaps it is a way to be there in spirit. I have painted a very beautiful painting for my parents' new home in Cambria, a quiet seaside village in central California, so that I can enjoy it when I go to recover from The Tidal Wave. It is a painting of La Reina del Mar, the Queen of the Sea. There are three mermaids in seashell-thrones engaged in peaceful everyday life under the water.

The thing that has really got me by the throat and the soul is that anticipating the end of this phase of my life I pulled down my last big canvas a few days ago and began to paint the Funeral of the Artist. It is the painting of the death and resurrection of various lifetimes. It is the wake everyone dreams of having, complete with a little meal of a man's head on a platter. You will notice he died with a smile on his face. Jeanne and I stand, admiring the debauchery, draped in mink. The Dark Man Who Waits is watching patiently in the wings. It is not yet his time. It is my death, this is the end. If he steps in too soon he will only be burned on the pyre—lost in the conflagration of transition. I have fearfully dreamt of him since I was a child. His time is coming, even in my dreams. In the painting are many old friends there to guard me, to guide me, to cheer me on into the next life.

WARRIOR WOMAN

What am I going to do? I have no idea whatsoever. I have no money and no plan. All I that I know how to do is to paint and paint and paint. I am done here. I must quickly complete this cycle of work, because I am dying. Even in two weeks I will be shot so far into my next life that this will no longer be relevant to who I am. The funeral had to happen now as a ceremony, to release me into the next experience. There is a new moon on Friday, and I must be ready to move. Unseen forces have plans for me. I can feel myself being passed from one hand to the next. Painting, I will surrender to that which is becoming. I am dying to who I have been.

My life is falling apart and yet I am happy. I am in a great deal of pain, but the pain will set me free. The pain is going to burn up the ropes that are tying me here.

October 13, 1986

My life in Los Angeles, City of Angels, is at an end. In a few hours the movers will come and move the adventure film of my life to Cambria. The last few weeks have been total disintegration interspersed with rage over Kelly's betrayal. So the benevolent society of movers, the Starving Students are on their way with a gilded gypsy wagon to take me to the next indicated life. I feel like hell. I am terribly, terribly sad.

My dear, dear buddies, Beth and Nan, have pretty much packed me up all by themselves. They're baby-sitting me until the movers arrive. We sit down in the bed every so often in a heap and cry. At least they're here. It hurts to leave all the love. It hurts to leave my life, which seemed so deep and rich to me all these years. I felt so secure and I left myself wide open to get creamed. I made a special farewell trip out to see Philippe to tell him that someone had done to me what I had done to him. I thought he should know that things had come full circle. Love is strange.

October 17, 1986

I have been living in the small coastal village of Cambria, which is exquisite, for three days. I have been lonely and confused. Deranged might be a better word. I am pretty cut off from my familiar support network, but today I shall have some company. Bob is coming from Santa Fe. We will go to one of my favorite places in the galaxy, Big Sur. I know this will be a journey of both breaking and building. There is a room reserved there in the Lodge with a fireplace. Lots of talking to do. Lots of crying to do, also.

A fireplace is a good place to start a friendship.

THE NIGHT
1980, housepaint on paper, 20" x 24"

WARRIOR WOMAN

October 20, 1986

The ocean. The oaks and firs. The cold night air. If you've lost everything, go to Big Sur to recuperate. The natural beauty there brings on a sort of rapture of the deep. We hiked all day, when we weren't on horseback riding wild down the beach. The fresh sea air washed over me and I could feel the pain of the last few weeks lift. If I were home again in Los Angeles, I would not be walking out under the moon and stars in Big Sur.

We rode on horseback through the ancient green forests, the cathedrals that are in abundance here. There was no concrete, only diffused green, and the crunch, crunch, crunch of the horses hooves. We rode through icy streams where the water came up to our ankles in the stirrups. There were smells of the rich earth, the hot leather, the piss and the sweat of horses. We cantered madly on racing horses. We came up over a golden rise to dizzying views of the sea. I have never seen the ocean bigger than in the Sur. At night when the moon is full, it is one of the wonders of the world to see—oceanic diamonds twinkling seductively, hypnotically as far as the soul can fly.

We hiked in primeval oak groves and swung through the branches. We fell to the ground laughing in the crackling golden leaves of many decades, many lives. We ate picnics and burned sage. We climbed into the massive arms of the ancient oaks and let the golden light bathe us in beauty. We climbed inside the massive trunks of the giant redwoods. We walked through the forests at night, listening to the conversations of owls. I had a good time.

October 25, 1986

A favorite student and friend from Los Angeles, Melissa Wye—just Wye to me—came for a painting safari in Cambria. We worked along the cliffs above the sea. I have never gotten such pleasure from the ocean before living here. There is time to just *be* there. Whole days can be spent enjoying the splendor of the water.

It's cold and we bundle up against the wind. We enjoy the sight of each other painting under a twisted cypress tree. We have had many marvelous expeditions painting together. She is a hard worker and has a wild set of playing cards inside of her imagination. We go to the bed rock mortars to sit and paint on the sensuous and welcoming rocks where Chumash Indians crushed their seeds and watched their children play in the pink and turquoise surf. We echo their lost laughter with our own, foam splashing all around us, onto our canvasses, into our tingling, wind-burned faces. We usually paint for three hours. We spend a great deal of time on the subject of wonderful food. We are also

46

dedicated to napping. The sun and the sea air zaps you. We wear stupid hats to paint in. I am glad for her company.

October 29, 1986

Nan has come to visit. We spent many hours walking along the winter beaches, which are mainly travelled by fellow Cambrians at this time of year. We climbed into the giant twisted pines that the area is known for. Settling into the crotch of the tree, we blabbed about everything until we were exhausted from the process. At night I took her to dance at one of the great saloons of all times, Camozzi's. I have a very odd friend here, Glen. We take him along as our body-guard. It is a wild place. We danced and danced until we dropped.

November 10, 1986

I've been to visit Santa Fe. I've been to every art gallery and museum in town. There is something that happens being around those adobe walls... I wanted to stay. Everywhere you look is something beautiful—the softened edges of the walls, the wooden gates, the art, the food! Oh my God! The food! It is a city for the sensualist. I loved it and I rolled in it and I feasted there.

The earth is red. You have to get out and lie down on it and soak in what it has to give you. It is grounding and vitalizing. The ground is full of bones from those who have lived there before. The sky is blazing blue, with a few Indian Yellow chamisa bushes vibrating against it. And the clouds! You can see how the Native American people believed the clouds were full of spirits. The clouds are surreally alive, dancing, dipping all day long. The light is crystal. I have never seen colors more clearly. The contrasts are completely absorbing to me. I love it there. I love the red dirt. It roots me back into the earth in a way that makes me want to create, to surrender, to pro-create.

Thanksgiving

Bob is gone to Europe. Mike is no longer a part of my life. I want to go home for the holidays, but I don't have a home anymore. Wye is here to paint. We're going to cook a Turkey. Things are looking bleak.

Chapter 7

STUDIO ON WHEELS
Notes from Sedona . . . Wedding of Fools in Santa Fe . . . Abiquiu . . .

December, all month, 1986

I seem to have gotten stuck in some kind of emotional time warp. I have essentially moved into my truck with Chile and my paints. I hope I don't kill her with the fumes. As for me, I would welcome an exit just about now. We wander from one city to another, trying to absorb the pain that is driving me. I sometimes try to force my way back to a home that no longer is there for me. I visit Don the therapist in Los Angeles, dipping down to see Jeanne in Indian Wells, out to Joshua Tree to paint with a group of students, or perhaps just Wye, then out to Santa Fe in a storm of tears and a fog of confusion. When people ask me where I live I say, "My Toyota."

I meet friends at strange, cracked airstrips in the middle of the desert, in Nowhere. I have a small bag of utilitarian clothes for my life in the Outback. I wash my clothes immediately wherever I spend the too-long nights and dry them in the sun while I eat breakfast over a map, preparing to run again. But necessities dry quickly hung out on a mesquite bush in the desert. Or out the window of my truck.

"When are you leaving?" people ask. I don't know. A few days, an hour, tomorrow, right now. I might have to leave in the middle of the night. All boundaries and definitions of myself have exploded. "Where are you going next?" I never know. The need to move on comes on me suddenly and there's no resisting. I have to just pack up and go. I get my map out and see where I feel like going and what I might like to see on the way.

My safe harbor has been blown up. There's only my dog and my car and my paints. There are shadowy movements in the wings to suggest that more will come, but it's no comfort right now. Right now I just want to find a place to rest for a few hours, to make a cup of tea, to visit with friends I miss desperately. What happened to my life? Where did it go? These are the questions more pressing to me. Was I wrong to love, to leave myself wide open? I guess it was the karma for my stupid and selfish destruction of my relationship with Philippe.

Christmas was a botch. I wanted to be with Kelly, but he couldn't have cared less — he was in Italy. I cried like a wretched thing. I scared my mother and father. I didn't know what else to do. I wandered in my car looking for some place where the pain would stop. I went out to Jeanne's for Christmas. I couldn't bear to have my parents see me in this condition. I needed to go to the desert.

48

After moping around Jeanne's watching the various happy couples, I finally gave in to Bob's pressure to join him in Santa Fe. I took off before dawn the day after a very painful Christmas and headed out into the wasteland to meet Bob at yet another ancient cracking airstrip in the desert. We'll go to Santa Fe. I want to go back to the home I loved. I don't want to give in to this man who is pursuing me. He makes me feel things that frighten me... I want to run away from him as fast and as far as I can.

January 5, 1987

I'm spending my life driving. Driving and painting. Sometimes when I'm driving across a huge, lonely expanse I'll see an intriguing rock formation. I stop and get out my paints, wrap myself in a blanket and get under a bush where I can work for a few hours. If you've ever lived as the prisoner of a city, the wide-openness of the country really makes you drunk. I can't get enough.

March 23, 1987, Sedona, Arizona

On my way through the desert between California and New Mexico I felt pulled to Sedona. I have never been here before. It is a place of tremendous power. It is a place to bring someone you are involved in a relationship with only if you have some courage. Everything accelerates here. The relationship either blows up in your face or progresses rapidly forward. So I have come here with Bob.

We have gone to the vortex near the airport. We felt the wind rising into our faces, lifting our hair. Our lips tingled from the vibrations there. It is a unique mix of strong energy and utter calmness. My dreams became more vivid and charged with meaning. We visited Bell Rock and hiked into Boynton Canyon. In Boynton Canyon the energy was so strong we acted as if we were stoned, wandering back and forth to the car for perhaps twenty minutes, forgetting various items we needed for the hike. I think we returned to the truck five or six times. We were drunk from the power of the earth itself.

We hiked far back into the canyon, admiring the red rock formations and each other. We sat for half an hour or so in our spot, just to be quiet, quiet. Sedona is a good place for us. We walked and talked and shimmered there. We told each other intense sexual secrets in the canyon, and made ourselves crazy with heat. Tomorrow we leave for Santa Fe.

WARRIOR WOMAN

April 1, 1987

I woke up this morning with a suitable performance art piece for April Fool's Day — a wedding. I proposed to Bob, and he accepted. We went out and bought a silver ring from one of the Native American street vendors in the plaza of Santa Fe. We hiked into the red hills in back of his house. I asked Chile to be my bridesmaid. She laughed and said yes. She likes Bob.

As we stomped up and down through the deep red arroyos looking for the place that felt right, we spoke about how we felt about each other. We talked about what it would be like to be together and what we would want in a marriage. It was not in fact an April Foolish discussion, but a very important negotiation-consultation. It was a good walk-and-talk, which is what we do to work things out between us.

Somewhere from the time we left the front door and the finding of the place that felt right, our April Foolery became very serious. We decided to make our own ceremony of commitment to each other. It would be like a trial marriage.

I took some pictures of us together looking sappy, and of my bridesmaid and myself in my wedding gift — a red blanket coat with the small metal milagros ting-ting-tinging, sewn on in profusion. I had my medicine bag with me and plenty of potently fragrant rosemary and sage for my wedding bouquet.

I've gone nuts since the wedding. I have experienced a tidal wave of anger. He got me! He trapped me! I don't want him to touch me, anywhere, or anyhow. The trickster! I hate him!

April 9, 1987, Abiquiu, New Mexico

Often when I am working I can't remember what year it is...

I came from Santa Fe to Abiquiu to paint today. As you drive through the minute town and out towards Ghost Ranch the earth changes dramatically. I stopped by the side of the road and painted some strange red stripey hills. Bob painted, too. Before we worked we drove to a place called the Echo Amphitheater, a place of whirling energies. We took in some of the scenery for possible painting locations. Then we screamed and howled — an excellent way to get ready to paint.

Abiquiu is O'Keefe country, and the difficulty painting here is that everything that you choose to paint in the landscape looks stolen. Finally I said screw it — just paint the red earth. Paint New Mexico. That's what I'm here for. O'Keefe painted the Pedernal, the red hills, the black place because these things gave her pleasure, I suppose. So we should all have the pleasure of losing ourselves in the land.

New Mexico is the kind of place you have to experience for yourself. It cannot be imagined just through the use of words. Bring your art supplies, your camera, paper to write on and all your warm clothes. Once you get here you probably won't want to leave. The land is enchanted and all the Old Ones still inhabit the mountains, the clouds, the rocks. The earth is rich with their bones.

The spirit of the land is still alive here, undiminished in power. The spirits draw you away from whoever you have been before, from all the things that you used to know or that once seemed to matter. There is both a forgetfulness that takes place and then a remembering.

Today I spoke to my therapist, Don. We had done a lot of deep work when I still lived in L.A. to get ready for changes I instinctively knew were coming. I am so terribly confused about what I'm going to do, where I'm going to live, wondering what is left of me. No resolution from the conversation, but a release by much crying. I miss Don and our wild inner journeying. We were a good spelunking team. I am pretty cut off from a large, well-developed network of support and comfort I have come to rely on over many years. Plus there is the grieving and shame over the loss of Kelly. If I want someone to cry with I have to get in my car and drive for four hours, six hours, fourteen hours. Consequently I live in my car.

For the last six months since things blew up in my face I have been living in my truck, wandering through the desert painting, crying, laughing, losing myself. It's the secret fantasy of many people — "Hey! I'll sell everything, quit my job, travel." Having a fantasy about walking away from your life is quite different from the realities of doing it! My exit was very freeing, but it also completely shut down the splendid momentum I had worked so hard to get going in my painting. It also left me without my studio or my life. Bang. Done. Yer out. I bought a computer to write with, but I have no electrical outlet in my Toyota. It still makes me real angry to think about it.

Since leaving Los Angeles I put my things into my parents' house and really started moving. I have been to Santa Fe several times, on pilgrimages to Chimayo and other natural holy places. Bob and I have explored Taos and all of its mysteries. I have been to Indian Wells I don't know how often to get my emotional tank filled at Jeanne's house and then up into the high desert at Joshua Tree to paint and give lessons. I still get time to paint, I'm just extremely portable. I have been rendered flexible by the great steamroller of life once again.

I painted some beautiful large paintings (4'x6') of the rocks and the haunted desert at Joshua Tree. One is now in a gallery in Palm Springs. I usually have stinking experiences with galleries, but I took it to them anyway. My money comes from the Great Spirit rather than from traditional sources. Also a little unemployment. When that's done, some more teaching. There is some income from long-term payment plans from painting sales. It works. I don't know how. I am far from starving and I always have a safe roof over my head — it's just always a different roof. I have become a child of the universe. A girl and her dog, wandering through a landscape destroyed by one of life's little nuclear blasts.

April 10, 1987

Often people ask me how I'm doing what I'm doing. What they really want to know is where do you get your money and how dare you do what you want? Well, my liberation was far from voluntary at the outset. And there are things much more important than where I get my money. The reality is a little more naked and distressing than a romanticized view of a life on the road. There is a desperation, but a certain groundedness to it all. The groundedness is a connection to the earth, my mother, and the Great Spirit because there isn't anything else. Then there is my work as an artist — because that's all that's left of my identity for my journey through the dark and creepy hallway between lives. And my dog who loves me completely and without holding back. She is a psychic companion for me also, often accompanying me in the dream world. Cerberus.

But there are some practical aspects of living on the road that are helpful. First, you get a five gallon jug full of water for your car. That comes before anything else. Then you get a p.o. box that will forward your mail to anywhere you call from. You hook up an answering machine somewhere in the country if you care to be reached, if there's anyone left to call. You get the kind with a beeperless remote so you don't need to buy batteries. All of that can be let go of pretty soon after you get rolling. You keep in touch with perhaps a few people. A few friends keep track of you, more or less.

You get everything portable — paintbox, easel, ice chest and food in the car (beef jerky, unsalted nuts, trail mix, rice cakes, peanut butter), camp stove, radar detector, a scary dog. I have a c.b. radio in my car — I'm the Desert Queen. I have a telephone credit card and credit cards for car repairs or medical emergencies. I pay for health insurance. Don't worry about getting your bills on time. They dope the computer chips now so you will get your bills even in the event of a nuclear disaster. So rest assured that with a few phone calls they'll keep the paper river flowing.

You won't lose your real friends. The ones who really love you will always keep a light burning in the window and a pot of soup on the back burner or accept an occasional collect call. You will, however quickly lose the insincere, the hangers-on. Not the gossips, though. They'll still speak of you often and at

52

length. You'll lose your identity, too. That's a bitch. If you've got any jewelry left at this point, leave what you can't wear in a vault or a pawn shop. Better leave your tiara, too.

I sleep where l can, where it's safe. I don't pay for my bed or meals with sex. I paint wherever I want for as long as I feel like it. I have supplies shipped to me at remote motels and unspellable spots on the map. Thank God for UPS. Every single detail of my life is different from seven months ago. Ultimately that is what makes it impossible to go back to where you came from.

Chapter 8

CONCEPTION
Surrender . . . Corn Dance at Cochiti Pueblo . . . Artists' group . . .
We find a home—or a home finds us . . . Dia de los Muertos . . .

April 14, 1987

Dream: I am lying on the ground out in the desert, naked. Loco weed is growing up all over me, ghostly white bells twining around my arms and legs. The flowers seductively open as the light of day is waning. I look closer and to my horror I realize that I am very pregnant. I wake up in a state of terror. I have never wanted to have a child or to get pregnant. I cannot let this man do this to me. Problem is that that's about all I can think about. Bob says it's the same for him. Oh God — what's happening to me?

April 23, 1987 Abiquiu, New Mexico

I am sitting high on a mesa overlooking Ghost Ranch, canvas propped, ready to paint. I am under a scrubby little juniper tree. It's important to find some shade, particularly if you're working out in the desert. Even tiny bushes provide some forgiveness from the killing hours of relentless sun. I paint in the morning, stopping around eleven, then perhaps go out again in the afternoon after two or three o'clock. You have your paintbrush in one hand and a camp cup full of water in the other. You drink and drink and drink, as much water as you can, or you get home and you don't know what's happened to you. You're desiccated.

Wye is here with me from California on a painting safari. We're out in the bush for three days and let me tell you, the vibrations are very weird out here. We have our four-wheel-drive vehicle, dog, five-gallon water jug and art supplies. We paint for a few hours, siesta, hike for a few hours, eat like horses and look like slobs. We sleep good — the deep sleep of the high desert. When I first started the art safaris I quickly decided to leave the costume changes at home. There is also no makeup, no nail polish. I cut my bangs in the rear-view mirror with my Swiss army knife. It looks like it, of course, but there's no-one out here to impress. I still pluck my eyebrows and shave my legs and pits, or you wouldn't be able to see me.

The silence out here is like a throbbing drum. One hears one's own blood coursing. You can hear the air itself, crickling and crackling with electricity and magic.

I'm working on a 30"x40" painting of the red and yellow cliffs, red rolling hills in the foreground, the hyper-real poofy clouds against a sky so blue it

54

Conception

makes me forget to breathe sometimes. The clouds are quintessential New Mexico. You could quite literally paint in just one spot for months or eons, turning this way and that, watching the clouds, the storms, the light changing during the course of a few hours and fill a museum with the variety of your work. People would think you were making it up.

April 30, 1987

Bob and I were out shopping today when I did some counting in my head. Disregarding the presence of the saleswoman I said, "If we go home right now we could get pregnant." The saleswoman chuckled. We quickly paid and split. We then went home and did the next part of the marriage ceremony — a seed planting party.

May 1, 1987

We went out to Cochiti Pueblo with Martha Littlebird today. Her daughter, Seracina, was with us. We went to see a Corn Dance in the heat and the dust, happy to be allowed to be there. The crowd was large and there were many dancers moving to the drum in the same ways that they have danced for rain, the corn, their crops and babies for centuries. A lead dancer came by us with a long pole. I asked Martha what he was doing. "Sprinkling us with metaphorical corn pollen." I knew my goose was cooked — that I was pregnant.

After the dance we walked along the bank of the Rio Grande. The cottonwood trees were dropping seeds into the wind. We were sitting in a shower of cottonwood seeds. We lay down on the ground and rested, talked. My body talked to me and I knew that I was a part of the whole process of renewal. Being in New Mexico has linked me up to a part of me that I have successfully denied all my life. It frightens me into near paralysis, but my body wants to surrender. I am no longer split into a body. A mind. Thwarted feelings. Aching spirit. I am whole, and I am part of the Great Mother earth herself.

The moon is full and I can't sleep. I am wondering if I am carrying a tiny baby inside of me now. It would bring my odyssey to a close. It would change me completely, yet once again. This will be a hard decision either way. There's no room in my truck for a baby. I don't know if there's room in my life for a baby or a commitment. Shitsky.

55

WARRIOR WOMAN

Too Mad to Know the Date

Woke up to find my car gone. In spite of our written agreement that he would pay for the car and put it in my name, Kelly had it repossessed during the night. This decides many things... I'm so mad I could kill. Helpless, too. But one thing he has definitely helped me with is to slam the door of indecision. I'm done there. I can perhaps forgive one betrayal, but not repeated treachery when I am at my most vulnerable. What am I going to do without my car?

It's noteworthy that when things turn bad with the men in my life, they immediately wound my father. He feels betrayed by Kelly. It hurts me to see his pain and disappointment. He thought of Kelly as a son. He also trusted him. Aren't we incredibly stupid to trust people? Right now it seems like it. He thinks Kelly owes us the money to buy the car — something other than an outright rip-off.

May 20, 1987 Cambria, California

It's not surprising that I have not gotten my period, is it? I am agonizing over whether or not to get a home pregnancy test — another boon to those of us who have chosen to live in our cars. I'm back and forth on the phone with Bob like a maniac.

A few hours later...

I am pregnant. Is there room in my car for a nursery? Oh, I don't have a car anymore. Is there room in my life for a child?

June 6, 1987

With the help of my father I picked up Voyager One, used van, new to me, on my way south to meet Bob in Palm Springs. I won't be stopping in Los Angeles anymore. Makes the trip shorter. Onward...

When the pain finally gets to Kelly, perhaps he will figure out that he owes financial amends to my family...

June 11, 1987, Santa Fe

After much inner struggling, we have decided to have our baby. Frequently I lapse into a state of utter terror. To my horror, milk already squeezes out of my breasts. My body has a strong mind of it's own. It is the very force of life itself, and I'm not going to try to fight it one more time. My body wants the baby. My heart wants to make a life with Bob. The war is over.

I feel centered here in Santa Fe. I feel calmer the moment I get out of the concrete cemeteries of Southern California and into the desert, the wasteland. It's quiet, and I am quiet inside. God can find me, and I can find my Mother-Father God. I can sit on a rock with my dog for hours, feeling the sun, feeling whole. There is no place to go and nothing to do. What I am is enough here.

I recommend this adventure to all my friends — quit your job and come wandering on the lunatic fringe. Here there is still a frontier, but the edges are in the interior. But there are few takers for this challenge. I ask too much. I was shot out here by catastrophe, and I suppose it is the only way one would choose to leave terra cognita behind. It's hard to get so far out in innerspace perhaps, without a little dynamite. One does not do this type of life by choice, rather one is chosen.

August 5, 1987

Have spent the last few weeks sicker than a dog who's swallowed a gopher, whole. Went to see the doctor (a woman, of course!) to confirm the obvious. Before we went I was afraid that she would tell me not to use my oil paints. "If she tells me I can't use my oils or ride a horse, I'm leaving." All went well. Ventilate well, she said — I always do. I do not actually feel like painting at this time — just throwing up. She also said I could ride horses, with restraint. No jumping.

August 15, 1987

Have found an interesting woman therapist. Her ad in the paper said she specialized in working with artists. Her name is Kronsky. I've had a few private sessions with her, spent mostly talking about my fears about being a mother and continuing my work and life as an artist. She had good suggestions about working on a smaller scale for now, i.e. in my book, and working using the subject matter at hand — being pregnant, terrified, whatever my feelings are at the moment. Not new suggestions, but helpful. I like her a lot.

I just don't know many women who have had a child and continued with their own lives, especially with regard to their art, after the birth. They just seem to give themselves up — they stop having lives of their own. The child seems to become the creative focus. The women cut their hair, put on their sweat pants and de-sexualize. Don't write me any letters — it's just the way it looks from the outside, through my terrified eyes. There's strong social coercion that one shouldn't want a life of one's own after having a baby.

WARRIOR WOMAN

People ask me what I do for work and when I say I'm an artist they chuckle. "You won't have time for that anymore." This is why I'm going to Kronsky. She swears it can be done. There is life after childbirth. There's just a shortage of role models. I'm paying someone to be my cheerleader. Whether she's right or wrong, I'm going to believe that I can do it. I'm going to be a mother and I'm going to go full speed ahead with my art.

August 25, 1987

Have been to the artists' therapy group. What a weird crew we are. There are some very wonderful artists who are also there for various reasons. We bring our work or photos sometimes to share with the group. There's plenty of crying and anger, the usual group dynamics of attention getting ploys, attacks against the therapist. I sit on the couch, big and pregnant, howling and dripping tears and sweat. The people are very supportive. The process is excellent.

I work in my black book regularly. I'm doing lots of smaller pieces, plus the painting of the dream where I am lying pregnant in the desert with the loco weed growing over me. You can see the bulbs and rocks down in the earth. The painting frightens me, but it is surely beautiful. It's "The Dream About the Mother." Being pregnant frightens me, but it is the most explosive learning experience I have had. I am round like the earth and just as full of life.

I wish that there were A.R.T.S.* meetings here. I need all the focus and encouragement I can get right now. After the baby is born I'm going to start one, even if it's in my own living room.

September 15, 1987

By a sheer miracle we have just moved into a hundred-year old adobe house in the historic district of Santa Fe. Our house is on a rise, so we look out across the city. There are three fireplaces, one in the bedroom, one in the studio. There is a skylight over our bed so we can watch the moon and the stars at night. And they can watch over us. I am in heaven. We have a clean, dry, safe cave now for our baby to be born. My cave-woman self is at peace.

October 31, 1987

Here it is Halloween — my favorite holiday of the year. I have bought myself some silver wings and a billowing white nightgown. I plan on going to the

---

* (Artists Recovery Through Steps, P.O. Box 175, Ansonia Station, NY 10023)

Halloween dance as a pregnant angel. Dancing is good for me, especially pregnant.

There are some very elaborate celebrations here in Santa Fe for the Day of the Dead. We plan on going to some performance art pieces at the Center for Contemporary Arts. Lots of exhibits with skeletons and corpses. I love it!

Our culture is so phobic about death. We are left completely at a loss when someone dies — it's something shameful, secret, cut-off. We all do it. No-one speaks of it. How can we participate in one of the most important events of our lives when it is a taboo subject? Drug the dying. Drug their family, the widow first. Few grieving people ever even cry in front of others — they need to be alone to feel their sadness. At funerals one is given points for holding in the feelings. It makes me sick and angry. I won't attend funerals. I don't behave in the American Way — I cry, noises come out of me, my nose turns bright red and drips snot copiously. I am destroyed in grief.

Anyway I revel in the celebration of death — the absurdity of the festive, grinning (leering?) skeletons. Halloween and Dia de los Muertos — these are two of my favorite days of the year. I am pregnant and we are dancing with death. I light candles and leave food out for my dead sister. I miss her, and on these days I visit with her. We are going out to the *baile* in my nightie and a halo. That's more like it.

Somewhere in December

Still going to Kronsky's group. It's been wonderful for me as an artist, and as a woman who is scared to death about having a baby. One night Kronsky said we would make a feeling map of the future. With my left hand I did a sketch of me looking into my baby's eyes. When I saw the image, I knew that all would be well. The love that I saw in the eyes was so radiant, all my fears that I might want to run away — or what would I do if I didn't like the baby, what if the parts necessary to mothering aren't in there? — all my fears dissolved. The painting told me the truth. The truth always calms me right down. Since then I have just focussed on the beautiful image. We have golden flower petals around our heads. We are in love. I have made an oil painting of the drawing. It's beautiful. Everyone wants it.

January 5, 1988

A few weeks ago it became imperative that I stretch a big (4"x5") canvas to paint on. I needed to start a painting I could keep working on through the birth of the baby. This was no small assignment since I am now as big as a barn. Laughing people stop me on the street and tell me so. How grateful I am to be pregnant in New Mexico where a pregnant woman is seen as sacred, beautiful and exalted. I could not have endured this experience in anorexic Los Angeles where one must be eighteen, blond, compliant and thin, thin, thin. Here men stop and tell me how beautiful I am and reverently ask if they might touch my belly.

Going to the art store and picking out my supplies has a new twist because I have to ask for help carrying the stretcher bars and the roll of canvas — something I never have to do. I want to do everything all by myself, and that's not even a remote possibility. It's a healthy balance for me when I have to ask for help. I can't remember the last time I had to ask—in lithography, I think. Pregnancy has been a course in interdependency for me. My ego could hardly stop choking on the words as I asked for help in many different situations.

Anyway, once everything was on the floor of the living room I set about stretching the thing, with a blimp attached to the front of me. There was much huffing and puffing and sweating. It was the hardest thing I have done physically in months. After twice the time it usually takes, the canvas was stretched and beautiful. I set it up on my easel to look at its white emptiness. My favorite thing! It makes me crazy with the drive to paint, to fill the empty space. I see a mental slide show whenever I stare at an empty canvas.

For perhaps fifteen minutes I stared at the white space and then I started "The Wind Spirits Over the Desert." I have been very afraid that I won't be able to get out into the desert to paint after the baby is born. The imagined confinement has rendered me frothing at the mouth, so I decided to send my spirit to fly over the land until I can get there myself. Just painting the red earth and the desert gets me high. My spirit is doing for me what I cannot do for myself right now. Being eight months pregnant I don't feel free to go out and paint far away, alone. I feel very vulnerable, and I am.

LEFT-HANDED SKETCH FOR MADONNA I
1987, ink on paper, 14" x 17"

Chapter 9

BABY IS BORN

The artist as mother . . . I don't want to die anymore . . .
Meetings for artists . . . Recognition as an artist . . .

February 14, 1988

Happy Valentine's Day, Tina. Last week on February 6, 1988, I gave birth to Alexandra Earll in Los Alamos, New Mexico, birthplace of the atomic bomb. I have been in the hospital a week because I had a Caesarean section.

Lots of people have asked how the birth went, was it "normal." Yes, it was normal. She weighed nine pounds, nine ounces. I had a c-section. They then will express their condolences. I think they're boobs — labor itself sucks, as far as I'm concerned. I was never so happy in my life as when the anesthesiologist leaned over me and said, "You're only going to have one more contraction." Yahooo! Let me out of here. Then quick as they could throw up a tent and roll up their sleeves, there's my little baby girl, radiant and howling! A miracle! Now this is life!

Shortly she was sucking on my tit like a vacuum cleaner — a pair of pliers — a hungry little bear. Her face looks most beautiful of all, right there on my over-ripe breast. She makes small hungry bear noises, too, and the noises soothe me. Bob spent the nights with us in the next bed at the hospital. We were a little tribe in our safe cave and all is well. Our child is a miracle — an angel sent to us.

I do not know how women have babies without the father being there with them at the birth. I was terrified — except even as I was losing it I knew that he was there at my side, looking deeply into my eyes, looking for me in the recesses of my animal being. I could trust him to do whatever I needed. He would get the job done. Pregnancy and childbirth are ancient experiences. The process accesses the cave woman inside of us, linking us to the mothers, the grandmothers, the ancient mothers, our mother, the earth. Bob made an excellent caveman, keeping a fire in the hearth and food on the table, watching through the night when I was gone into the other worlds. He wept in helplessness, and I wept in gratitude for his courage to be there.

I haven't felt like painting yet. I hardly feel like getting out of bed. Just a little walking and a lot of sucking. My tits are the size of watermelons, they hurt like hell from being too full of milk, and they drip everywhere. Fortunately the little bear is ravenous. And I do mean ravenous. So for now I am creating milk rather than working in my customary medium of oil. I call the baby Milky Face.

When I was in the hospital I had a shocking intuition. I felt that I would be losing one or both of my parents soon. It was as if nature had tricked me into having a child to root me to the earth, to ground me when the grief comes. I felt panicked. Have I betrayed my parents?

February 16, 1988

Health care pros and other medical authorities tell you that a baby can't focus her eyes for a few weeks, but Alexandra looks most intently at all my big paintings. Her eyes are drawn to them, and we hold her up so she can study the canvasses. I play classical music for her, Chopin and Debussy, which I also did when I was pregnant. She likes to look through the skylight in our bedroom at the clouds sailing by. I like her as a person.

In the hospital in Los Alamos (the nurses in Santa Fe were on strike) I had the most extraordinary nurse, Sage Kimbal. She gave me a crash course in the week that I was there. She initiated me into the Model Mothers of America. I learned later that she takes people on vision-quests. God knows she was there for mine. She has come to visit us at home, thank God. Between her and our beautiful nurse, Joy, I am learning how to take care of a baby and myself at the same time. How lucky I am to have such people around me. It feels like I am with the women of my chosen tribe. They are close at hand to support me, to help me after childbirth, to find my own way to be a mother. I am with the strong women, full of wisdom and experience. They gently encourage me to do this mothering thing in my own way. When I left the hospital with Bob and the Alexandra, the nurse who wheeled us out said, "Now don't be afraid. When you don't know what to do, just be quiet and listen for the answer to come from *inside.*" That's what I do well.

March 5, 1988

I am painting again! I put the baby in a little fuschia-colored sling and she snuggles right up next to me while I work at the easel. She intently watches the brushes moving and the colors flying. She is small enough right now that I can nurse her while I'm painting. Now that's a high!

Time and energy are at a premium. It's easier to write in short spurts....

March 11,1988

We found a beautiful cradle basket with handles — a Moses basket. I painted today at the easel with Alexandra next to me in her basket, bundled up in a bright Pendelton blanket. She is mesmerized by the painting process. I have been able to work at a stretch of forty-five minutes, which is excellent. I can get a lot of work done in forty-five minute increments. She gazes sometimes at the painting I'm working on, and other times at the yellow forsythia waving outside the French doors in the studio. It's a beautiful scene!

I started a painting of a woman with her new child, sitting on the red road that is winding through the golden chamisa. I had a hard time letting myself paint this subject. It seemed too soft, too female! Where does that shit come from??!! The wiser side of me said, "Paint what's important to you now. If you don't paint this experience that means so much to you, you will miss part of it, diminish it. It is one of the best times you will ever live. Paint it. Paint everything, every nuance. Paint it all you want." The internalized Woman of Wisdom, after all the years of wise teachers...

April 3, 1988

Sometimes I think about dying now. It is very different from before. I used to want to die more than anything, even as a small child. As I went along in my life the pull became clearer, stronger, more seductive. I flirted with dying whenever the opportunity presented itself — dangerous men, driving drunk, crawling through bad parts of the city alone at night, drunk and drugged to the hilt. I wanted to embrace my death like a lover in the dark — a little spooky, but very exciting.

Now my growth has played a trick on me. Years spent in nearly constant emotional pain have receded like a long tide. I am with a man who loves me, whom I love. I have a child who is an angel, a radiant being, full of light. I don't want to die anymore.

I wonder when I do die, what will become of my child, who will care for her? But the Great Mother, the earth, will care for her. I will hand her over to her and she will look after my child when it is time to let go.

Mother's Day, 1988

"Sasha" — that's what we call her now. We had a day alone together. I packed her up and we went to the art museum. It was incredible! My first Mother's Day — me and my baby at an art museum, checking out everything. When we would get in front of the big paintings I would pick her up and scan her back and forth so she could absorb the painting, the color, the texture, the feeling. She gazed intently, and chattered loud baby talk to the paintings. When we did this, crowds gathered to watch.

Baby is Born

My mother always hated Mother's Day. No present, please, no card. To me it's a very, very big deal. I wanted to celebrate it in a momentous fashion, and we did. I'll always remember this first Mother's Day. I bought myself a bolo tie as my first Mother's Day gift.

Mid-May, 1988

We had our first A.R.T.S. meeting in my living room today. This is a group based on the twelve steps of Alcoholics Anonymous for artists, writers and all creative people who want to make a greater commitment to their art, get past some blockage, or find their creativity if they haven't done so yet.

There were several other new mothers and all types of folks that wanted to get going with their art. There was a dancer, a weaver, a drawer, a musician, a jeweler, and me. There were also four new and nearly new babies at our meeting, slurping, screaming and cooing.

We plan on having childcare (paid for by voluntary donations in a basket that we pass) as a regular part of the meeting, so I told everyone to just bring their babies, and we would learn to concentrate with them there. There are some imaginary unspoken rules in the art world — i.e., women should stop doing their art, at least for awhile, when they have had children. If you choose to have a child then you are not a "serious" artist. If you have a child you should run out of the room if the kid starts crying — drop your artist hat and put on your mother hat. So we are going to integrate our babies into our lives as artists. Anyway, I am. Let me tell you, these kids are noisy.

We will continue to meet at my house until we find a more public meeting place with a suitable room for the kidcare. A.R.T.S. was a powerful program for me in Los Angeles, and I want more of the juice that it delivers, especially now that so much has changed in my life. I want the internal spiritual structure that it takes to keep on expanding and growing, rather than deleting important parts of myself. I need to be firmly hooked up to the unlimited source.

I am very, very excited to have an A.R.T.S. meeting in my life again.

One week later

We have a timer in our meeting so that everyone gets to share equally. It's funny how when you have a group, some people are so sneakily adept at dominating the time, even little mousy-types that you think have nothing much to say — then, twenty minutes later you are hoping to shove a stick of dynamite up their behinds to get them to shut up. Then you realize that they are doing this week after week. So we have a timer. The people who either a) know everything or b) can't shut up always object strenuously to using a timer. Dividing up the time so that every single person attending shares at every get-together keeps the meeting healthy. What every person has to say is as important as the next person. People really change by participating in every meeting. Every week people think they have nothing to say, or they're afraid they'll say the wrong thing. Some think they'll sound stupid, while others simply don't get their hands raised. Sharing at each meeting, they find out that they are enough. They find their voice, and then their courage. Finally they find themselves.

This whole process of sharing every week is like teaching a woman that she should have an orgasm each time she makes love. She has a right to want it, to go after it, to get it. It's the same obstacle course that artists have to run to get themselves to do their art, so I think that it's essential that they run the gauntlet right there in their weekly meeting. If they can learn to share their feelings in a meeting, it's a habit that shows up in their work.

September, 1988

There is a wonderful show at the Armory for the Arts, and I am in it! It's called the Recovery Show — for anyone who is in "recovery" — whatever that means to them. The work is full of feelings and passion. I am so happy to be included. The opening party was lovely, and it was totally jammed with people. I sold my painting, "The Dream About the Mother." There is a beautiful photo of my "Self Portrait in Transition" in the Santa Fe Reporter. I am ecstatic!

October 13, 1988

Everything is going to change. My lizard brain is warning me to get ready. In fact, we were driving down the dusty dirt road to our house when I got one of those messages that I get: "Everything is going to change. It's not your imagination. Everything is going to change. You are going to lose a lot, but don't be afraid. It's going to be replaced by things that are better." What do you do with a message like that?

I'm going to start getting together as often as I can with the women I have been working with here in Santa Fe, and try to pass on everything that I can before the tidal wave hits. They think that I'm dying, but I'm not. It's a big change that's coming, though.

Chapter 10

THE RED ROAD

My father dies . . . We are uprooted from Santa Fe . . .

December 5, 1988

We are visiting my parents in a community that I hate in California. They have just moved here, and the place feels bad to me. My father is drifting during the days. He's not as much a part of us as he used to be. We don't try to pull him back. He wants to be left alone more than before. We'll stay for a couple of weeks. Kris, my beloved niece, and her husband, Carlo, are visiting too, and I am happy to be near her. It is the first time we have all been together in years, and possibly the last.

December 20, 1988

I have been working on a painting of me holding the baby, out on a mesa with the red road that we all walk on. We have haloes of yellow sunflower petals all around our heads. The painting is just about finished. I have an pressing need to put some bones on the red earth next to us. I'm fighting with myself — put the bones in, leave them out-because it's such a disturbing element in the serenity of the painting. But I know in the end it is something that must be said, so I give in and paint the skull and the bones. That's what the dance is — new life standing on the bones of those who came before — birth and death, all in the same frame. It is a haunting painting.

January 15, 1989

We were on a weekend business trip to Tucson when the call came from my mother, "Can you come? Your father is acting strangely." I put Sasha in the car and we drove across the desert. On the phone my father told me he was dying.

January 16, 1989

My father is in the hospital. He is hallucinating wildly. He talks of the umbrella parties that the nurses have, and of their advances towards him. He knows me and the baby, but his mind is fleeing this world. I stroke his hand, I pretend to joke with him, but I know this is the thing that I have dreaded for so long. I tell him often that I love him. He is in this reality less and less with every passing hour. There's little to give him but love.

January 21, 1989

My witty and brilliant father who has loved me so much all my life is now a loudly howling vegetable. I hope he will die and die soon so that this torture does not have to go on one moment longer than it has to. I wonder if he is aware of what's happening to him? It's the most horrible thought. The doctors tell me no, and I pray that they're right. Oh to be in Santa Fe in the care of my friends. Or in Indian Wells in the arms of Jeanne. I don't sleep much. There is no place to get away from the pain here. I hate this place.

February 4, 1989

He is gone. It didn't really take so very long for him to die — two weeks. The time seemed much longer to me.

February 6, 1989

Sasha is one year old and healthy. She still nurses, and that stops the unending pain. There is great joy in being around her. She has a way of dragging me back to the land of the living. Everywhere else is hurt. We all watch her all the time.

February 8, 1989

We thought we were only going away for the weekend. I do not see how I can leave my mother here in this black hole in California. We are going to put our house in Santa Fe on the market and take my mom to Kingman, Arizona. She is too sick too come up to the seven thousand foot elevation of Santa Fe, she says stubbornly. If I don't do this I am afraid she will die of a broken heart. Or I will be spending the next few years driving back and forth across the desert from New Mexico to California fixing things for her and trying to give her love long distance.

I don't want to do this — live with my mother in Kingman, and at the same time I do. Bob and I love the desert so, and have spoken of trying to buy a big house there. We could enjoy the desert and just paint and write. We're leaving in a few days to go find a house there. I have to get out of this place as soon as possible.

Since we weren't expecting this, I am stranded without my art supplies. I have called the house sitter and asked her to ship me my oil paints, my French easel that collapses, and my camera. It's expensive to ship them, but I don't know how long we will be stuck in this place that I hate. I also know that my mental well-being depends on my being able to paint, so it's well worth it. I'll set up in the garage to paint in so I can have some privacy. With a garage door open there's always plenty of light and ventilation. It will give me a place where I can be alone.

I want to paint a picture of me nursing Sasha. I feel that she is coming to the end of this phase of her life, and I want to have a feeling — record of this, because it is surely one of the most beautiful things I have ever experienced. In the painting we are sitting out among the mesas. Big white jimson weed bells surround my head like a cloud. It has to be an especially beautiful painting, and especially soft as well. As soon as the paints come I will start.

Chapter 11

THE MESAS OF KINGMAN
Grieving . . . A new life . . .

March 18, 1989

On May 15th we'll move to our new house in Kingman, Arizona. I am extremely uncomfortable here in Nipomo. It's the place of my Dad's death, and God knows what happened here in the history of the Chumash Indians. It's a dark place disguised as a wholesome golfing community. I am depressed and it is almost impossible to make myself work. I am lonely for my friends, but they are all far away, some in more ways than others. I am in a state of serious crisis with one friend I have shared with like a sister for years. The loss of the relationship is devastating. Wye came to visit, which was a bright spot.

We will never go back to our warm and cozy cave in Santa Fe, the place where our baby came home to, a warm fire burning in the kiva fireplace next to our bed, the place of much joy and closeness. I am heartbroken by the loss of our home and my dad. It's very hard to recapture that happiness now, cramped in a house that I hate in a town that I don't particularly care for. I long for the high, open desert, the lilacs blooming soon in Santa Fe, the cottonwood trees cascading seeds over our heads. I miss our home and am lost under waves of feelings that I don't like. In bed at night when I am cuddled up next to Bob, all is well until we fall into the fitful sleep of the exiled. Each morning I wake up more exhausted.

I am hanging on until I can get to the Mohave desert, where Kingman is. The house is set off alone surrounded by beavertail, creosote, Spanish bayonet, strangely colored bushes peculiar to the arid land. All around there is nothing but sky, sand, mesas, clouds, space. I know there will be relief for me there. I know the land will comfort me. I want to paint the mesas.

The mesas in Kingman are fascinating to me. You can still get a sense of the people who once lived in and around them. The Hualapai Mountains are across the valley from our house, sensuously changing colors in a chameleon-like fashion throughout the day. They are pink, then blue, then purple, then pink-orange, all in an hour. The sunset falls 360% here. I want to sit outside and stare at the land, wander into the canyons and down the twisty trails. I get little comfort from the company of people right now. I need to drop some tears out on the Mother, out where I can hear the voice of the Great Spirit.

April 29, 1989

It is my Dad's birthday today. There's no respite from the sad feelings. I am just trying to hang on by a thread until we get to Kingman in May. I've got to get out to the desert to heal as soon as I can.

The ocean, which used to be a great comfort, doesn't work for me anymore like the empty lands to the south and the east — the Mohave, the Sonoran, the Great Basin. The desert is a drug! Once you have gotten hooked on the open spaces of the Southwest, that's all you can think of. I once thought that I could never leave the Pacific Ocean. Now I feel the same way about the desert. It is an ocean of emptiness. When I leave it for any length of time I long for the searing heat, the dryness, the howl of coyotes outside my bedroom window, the sea of stars. I must go where I can see the shooting stars and the cactus bloom. I've got to go where I have to search for life between the cracks in the seemingly dead earth.

June 19, 1989

We are in Kingman now. It's hot and getting hotter. I have set up a beautiful studio in a large open room off of the area where we sleep. I am working on a painting of the mesas which I can see when I open the garage door. They are all blue and purple and moody. I got lost in the colors of the desert bushes, which are almost impossible to paint at first, then almost impossible to stop painting.

I am in another life, but my little tribe is together. That is a novel experience for me!

I had a strange dream. I was in bed with Bob, making love wildly. I looked up and saw my father standing in his boxer shorts as if he were drunk, up on a balcony. He was screaming at me to stop that. I became even more frenzied in my pleasure, opening against all inhibitions. My father began to falter, then waste away to nothing.

There is an old part of me that tells me that I have betrayed my father by falling in love with a strong man, becoming a woman rather than his daughter, letting go of the ties that held me to my father. In that betrayal I released my hold on him that kept him alive. It is the belief of a child of alcoholic parents. It makes me sad and it makes me angry.

It is hard for me now, to process feelings like that. The meetings here are ineffectual, at best. I don't have any friends to share with, to unburden with. What I am carrying is too heavy for my husband to help with right now. In a six week period we lost my dad, Bob's mom, and his beloved step-daughter was found dead in an alley of a drug overdose — dumped there by her friends. We left our home that we loved in Santa Fe for a weekend and never saw it again. He has his own sadness and anger to deal with. We have little to give each other now.

I feel guilty for being such a wreck. Isn't that a mean thing to do to yourself — to beat yourself up when you're down?

July 28, 1989

Seems to me the trouble comes when you start to think about how to begin. I mean, I've been trying to get back into this damn book for over two years. First, it was the disruption of moving from my studio and my life in Los Angeles. Then it was wandering in the desert painting and adventuring for a year. In 1987 I was pregnant. The best I could do was paint and make a few sporadic entries in my drawing journal. In 1988 Alexandra the Great was born. I put the baby in a basket at the foot of my easel and showed her how to paint. Unless I keep up working steadily on this journal, a book is never going to happen.

This year I finally toodled over to get another Mac... the artist's dream of a computer. Sometimes you just have to put your plastic where your mouth is and buy it. If you haven't managed to get a credit card yet, you're going to have to go back to Creative Credit 101. Artists need credit.

So this year I find myself with a large familial entourage in Kingman, Arizona. There isn't an "Art World" in Kingman. This morning I dropped off a nice press packet to a reporter at the local paper, hoping to entice her to write an article about my art. This type of thing is not easy for me. I read a chapter in Kenneth Harris' *How to Make a Living as an Artist*, followed the directions, winged it, and put it on her desk before I had time to think. It's the only way to get anything done.

I have my paintings hanging on the walls of the local bank in the historic district of Kingman. I asked the Mohave Museum if they would give me a solo show. I'll enter the local contest to get a painting on the cover of the telephone directory. My work looks very different from that of the other artists in the area. That's a great advantage but it can also be a great disadvantage.

Thing is, there's nothing else to entertain myself with here. I paint a lot. The house is set back in the mesas. Whenever I look out the windows I get the itch to paint what I see out there. I have set everything up to make it easy to do that. My easel is set up at the foot of my bed. I go to sleep and wake up to the piece I'm working on, or the mesas, or the full moon flash-flooding through the windows. It's The Desert. There's nothing else like it. The mesas and the floor of the desert vibrate with energy. The coyotes perform an opera every night. There's nothing to do but talk back to them.

July 30, 1989

Now the extraordinary thing is that this very wonderful reporter has called me back rather than driving by the house and lobbing a brick through my window. Tomorrow morning we'll make an appointment to do a feature. There are certain advantages to being in a small town — like journalistic enthusiasm over something besides cows. I like cow journalism, though. Beats the usual metropolitan rape-a-thon, which makes a woman want to run screaming with her tiny daughter out into a cave with a gun and a mean dog.

This evening I've been trying to crystallize some of the things I want to say during the interview. There's always that niggling question of what do I say if she asks me where I went to art school. In some situations I think I need to be completely defended with smart-ass lines that will quiet that question forever. The world of academia often likes to humiliate those of us who were too busy doing our work to spend four years doing what other people told us to do. I have a great aversion to being told what to do, how to do it, when to have it in, being judged and graded by someone else's standards. Still, there is a certain safe feeling from going along the well-worn path that I miss sometimes.

The more I look at other people's work in a cold, objective way, the more powerful my work and the more valid my path seem to me. The paintings are very centered, full of feeling, with the unconscious intruding and invading just enough to give it real, surreal LIFE. My paintings are alive to me. Sometimes I see them breathing. I paint the way I want to paint, and I work on the pieces until I like them. I could only learn that by being art-self-centered, not centered or directed or affected from the outside.

This is one of the things I am always looking for in other peoples work — power, strength, truth, guts. It's what I admire and that's what I'm looking for in my own paintings that I value — Guts! It's so hard to find proper descriptive words for art that haven't been overused, that do not become cerebral and distance us from really feeling the art...

So anyway I am thoroughly complimenting myself, as I believe all artists should, since damn few others will, for resisting the conveyer-belt method of producing artists via art schools. I didn't go because a) I was too busy painting, b) I was afraid I couldn't conform, and c) I was afraid Nurse Ratchet would be teaching my class. But every time I go to a show I sneak a look at their bios and notice They Have All Been to School. Always look for the differences when you're determined to prove that you're inferior. I have considered lying, but I can't.

Anyway, I have this desire to become a landmark in the city of Kingman, and in fact upon the very face of the earth. The drive is very strong. I paint and struggle for recognition. There must be a way to get all those paintings out of their crates and up on the walls so that people can study them, get lost in them, find their way in them. I would like to get my hands on a building and turn it into my own museum where the work can be seen.

It is a most inspiring thing to the process of individuation to spend time with an artist or any other dreamer who has stayed true to her vision. Brave people went before me and showed me that it can be done. I want to do it for me and for all those who come after, especially my own daughter. "May she never be forced to bend under the will of another." This sentiment was uttered as my spiritual wish for the newborn daughter of the Littlebirds in a smoky sweat lodge on a snowy night in the Sangre de Cristos. I want the same for my daughter and for all the rest of us "locas."

I'm going to drop off the edge of this world right now. Whatever comes out of my mouth tomorrow will be just right. Perhaps it is best not to approach it as the last interview I will ever be asked to give. But again, thanks to the Dorothys, Sueo, Arnold, and all the rest who went before.

August 7, 1989

After all that self-torture and angst the reporter came over and we did an interview for about two hours. She took photos, I didn't sweat or need to act like someone else. So it just goes to show I was wrong. You can get some good out of an exhibit in a bank. It can be newsworthy! The interview was a joyful experience. Susan Allred. She was someone you could really communicate with. I didn't tell her I read The Enquirer regularly.

Thank God I can actually paint and write so I have something to show for about twenty years' investment... crates and crates and crates. When I move, it's like relocating Count Dracula. I can be cremated, but what the hell is my family going to do with The Crates? Finally, it will be someone else's problem.

I tried to go into etching for a few years. I bought a Black Book, 4"x6" format, for sketching. But I found that I was in fact making perfect preliminary drawings for giant paintings. The prelims would incubate in a neat matchbook size drawing, but when I went to paint these perfect little gems it was necessary to paint them the size of, oh say, a king-size bed. California king. Thus the damned packing crates. I need some elephants to move them, along with the tent for my travelling circus.

Anyway, as an update, I am no longer an artist. We have been taking care of the baby, who's now eighteen months old, and I am a total wreck. We usually invest a good part of our earnings on child-care, but it doesn't seem to be so easy to find many caregivers in Kingman without tattoos (You tattooed the baby's what?) and Harleys. Anyway, speaking for myself, I'm ready for a nice convalescent home. Hurricane Sasha. When I have some time to myself — which I used to fritter away painting-I dive for the eiderdowns. It was nice being an artist and all, but now I am sleepy.

If you're in this spot, do what I did. Rush to the classified ad department and beg for help. That's how this is coming out. I'm using the last ration of my energy to write this before I fall flat on my face.

August 20, 1989

Started work on a new painting yesterday. Two are in progress. The older painting was started in Nipomo, where my father died, the place I hate most in the world. Some good work came out of that hole though. It usually does.

The painting is a record of the feelings I had/have about Alexandra nursing. We are in the desert under the mesas. She is suckling and I am looking down at her. We are draped with jimson weed. I went out into the desert evening with my little sketcher's stool to watch the white bells of the jimson flowers open up once we got here. It's one of those paintings it takes a long time to develop. I have to spend a lot of time just looking at it on the easel at the foot of my bed. I do a little here, a little there, and stop.

The next painting in that series is the one I started yesterday. In the painting the woman is with her child sitting out in the desert looking at the sky, which has both the coppery lunar eclipse of last week, as well as the coming solar eclipse. The jimson weed is wrapping all around them and there are ocotillo cactuses scattered throughout the desert. I worked on it for about it for an hour so I could just get the first layer of paint all over the canvas.

All this is fine and well. I am painting, I am writing. But I am still going through my life in a half-dead state. I wander around in a deep state of grief over the death of my Dad. Even as I write this many images of his piercing blue eyes and his beautiful face flood my mind and my heart. It's hard to write, but I want to pull a little bit more of this out of the plumbing. The blockage is making it very hard to feel, to paint, to make love, to be happy. Tears are like that. They have to come out.

I see him laughing, smiling. I hear him talking to me. I want to call him, kiss him, tell him stories of our daily life — dog stories, baby stories, stories about my adventures as an artist. I cannot bear the knowledge that he and I will never speak again. Maybe he will reach me at some time, but now I feel that he is far, far from me. He went far away before he died and his soul did not linger close to us. He was really done, and he really left, and there is no place to put the love and attention I reserved for him. There are other people that I love: Bob, Alexandra, my mother, Jeanne, but he is gone and nothing can ease that pain. No one fills the place inside of my heart that he filled.

I know that he would have loved it here in Kingman. At times that pleases me and other times that causes me terrible pain. He never will see it. How are we supposed to go on in life as the people we love are taken from us? I cry everywhere, but few people have anything useful to say. No one discusses the subject. It frightens them. I frighten them. My feelings frighten them. Maybe no-one dies for them, I don't know. They act as if one should go into the bathroom and lock the door to grieve. So I'm lonely. I must be the only person who falls apart in the world. Bob lost his mother at the same time that Dad died. He says little. She was dead for him a long time ago.

I'm writing all this in the hope that this will dislodge the log-jam inside of me. I feel the difference and see it in my work when I am willing to listen to the people inside of me who have something to say. Very often it is "off the subject" at hand, but I feel that these messages are the real subject of life — out of my control. Unless I am willing to listen, nothing else can get through. I look like I'm living, I'm breathing, but I am slowly choking just the same.

It kind of goes along with my Feeling/Creating/Sex Theory: When I'm blocking one of my circuits, none of the others work. They all are on the same wiring. So I've learned to take care of all of these areas. When one isn't working, like say, my sexuality after I've had a baby, I CAN'T STAND IT. I get so mad I can't talk. I can't talk and then I can't paint. I can't paint and I'm so blocked up that finally I can't feel so don't touch me, I'm reading. This happens to me pretty frequently, and I haven't figured out all the ways to short-cut the process except copious crying on a regular basis. Which is what I'm doing. I wish I had a bandana. You can get an unbelievable amount of snot into a bandana — maybe a full hour's worth of it. It doesn't leave your nose all red and glowing in the dark. I don't have one — toilet paper is second best. Kleenex is too small for a real crying fest...

I hear the baby waking up. Someone has been sent from God to help with the baby and the house. This costs us about as much as renting a house but if you want to do some serious creating it is a fact of life: don't clean your own house. Scrape together whatever money you can find and have someone come help you. When they're there run, don't walk, to your work place and Do It. I thought I was going to die of exhaustion before help could be found. I was feeling weird and guilty about this ("Other people do raise kids by themselves." "How can I justify this when we have so little money?") until she got here. Then I was able to sink to the floor in relief. I slept and slept for the first time in weeks. The truth is I need a lot of help. I need a network of people to help me, and all the guilt, embarrassment or shame in the world is not going to alter that fact one iota. So get the fucking help! I was able to begin painting and writing shortly after reaching this surrender.

August 31, 1989

A brief comment on the date before each entry in this manuscript: I just put any date in that seems right in the heading. I never have an accurate idea of the generally agreed upon date, so I just pick the one on my watch, which is always incorrect, or I add or subtract a day or two according to the warp in my perception of reality. Poetic license. It's the wrong day. No, it might be right today. I make a point of not keeping track. It's not Monday, I know, because I hate Mondays and I always know when it's Monday.

September 25, 1989

I wish that I could paint something — anything! I wanted to put that in for the benefit of those who think I don't have a hard time getting going. It is enough to make me scream when everything is plugged up inside of me. The worst of it is that this is a time when we are so tight financially that we are going to have to go to our old standby of black beans and rice to be able to buy enough groceries this month. I'm so sick of being tight financially I could pull my hair out. Shut up and pass the beans.

There's a lot of truth to the "Stay Hungry" theory. Anyway I'm going to put it to work this month. It's like if you're a little bit hungry you get very creative. I put an ad in the paper for "three special students." I got a nine-year-old girl who's a delight to work with, and a ten-year-old boy whom I haven't met yet. Of course while I was working with the little girl I set it up so I work too. That was the first breakthrough I've had for awhile. Been a few weeks. Too long.

Since there's not a support group here for artists, I want to try something with my journal as an experiment. I want to make a commitment to go out with either my sketchbook or a canvas to work out of my car, out in the desert. I am surrounded by many of the most beautiful rock formations, mountains and mesas I have ever seen. They have not been painted to death, a la New Mexico. It is one of the things I know that I can do that will make me feel better about my sentence to the land of Neanderthal thought.

I want to try making a commitment here in my journal to see if it will help me focus my efforts like the commitments I used to make in A.R.T.S. meetings. It was a very effective tool — committing to a certain task, returning the next week and talking about my experiences — i.e.: Did I fulfill my goal or not? Besides working outdoors, I want to prepare my slides for submission into the Arizona Artists' Slide Registry, and replace my ad in the local paper to try to dig up a few more students. There's a time deadline on the slide submission, so I guess I better do that first.

The application for the slide registry is intimidating. There are parts for "Education," now that art is totally legitimate, no bastard sons; the part for "Awards" when you haven't had any; and "Grants" when you couldn't qualify if you slept with the people who gave them out ("Let me show you a real performance art piece."). Blank, blank, blank. Let's see — I've got an arty name! My application, when completely filled out, is almost as empty as before I started.

Well, I'm going to fill it out and send the frigging thing in anyway. I don't have the money right now to shoot my recent work, so I said to hell with it. I'll send in what I already have. If they're accepted I'll invest in some more photography. This stuff gets really old, tedious and hard. Maybe it wouldn't be so old, tedious and hard if it wasn't for all the rejection. I really wonder sometimes if my ship is going to come in, or if it simply vaporized in the Bermuda Triangle...

Over the years I have had a lot of encouragement and pep talks from my friends, teachers, family and supporters. But it is really hard just right now to keep it up and not just give in, sliding into the nice, warm ooze of housewifery and motherhood. Oh hell, that's bullshit. I have a very strong drive to get my work out where it can be seen by people. I also have a tremendous drive to be very successful. I know I can do it if I just keep painting and sticking my neck out there.

I can't stop that drive even sitting in a major depression with another rejection slip in my hand, waiting for the next good idea and the next influx of nerve. Then back to the phone calls, the letters, the endless dead-end interviews with people who can barely conceal their annoyance or boredom.

There is an unspoken rule in life to not reveal such insecurities. They are shameful. I sound bitter to myself — like a loser with a bad attitude. The only way out of the spiral is the truth. I hate this part. I am sometimes totally discouraged and negative. My first husband left me with many a parting shot about what a loser I was, and there are many days when I am afraid that he was right. I am also afraid that a lack of confidence really does make it harder to reach the next level of success. But I can't just shove the feelings under a chair and think that if no-one else sees them, and I don't admit it, they won't affect me.

OH SHIT. It's Monday, you see. The committee was waiting for me when I woke up. Don't think that this stuff gets any easier when you're married or partnered. Other demands are simply stacked on top of your own. I am sitting here with a file full of rejection slips and a stack of bills in the glamorous world of art. Arrgh. Enough. I can't hold up any longer under the avalanche of my own negativity. Healthier to go out for a hike.

October 1, 1989

Well, I've completed all the hunting and gathering work required to submit my photos to the Arizona Commission on the Arts Slide Registry. When I wrote last time I hadn't looked at the entry. I had forgotten how formidable it was to me. I winged it, and filled in where I could. I believe it is an unjuried selection, but I have no confidence that my work will somehow wind up in the slide registry.

Some of the things I do, I just do for the experience. I try all the avenues that look even slightly appealing. I follow through on my commitments that I make to myself on these pages. Before I close tonight I'll need to look back to the date on my last entry to see how long I have to go out in my car for an art outing.

There is something else I need to do before Wednesday afternoon, and that is to call the woman in charge of exhibits down at the Mohave Museum. I called her some time ago to request a solo show of my work. The work they show there now is local and simple, but I have always wanted a show in a museum. Why not the local Kingman museum?

Of course I have great trepidation about going to ask for such a thing. But I am going to try it anyway. What have I got to lose? I intend to call her sometime this week, just so I won't feel like it's one of the things I would have liked to try but didn't have the guts to stick my neck out. I also can't think of anything in the realm of self-promotion that doesn't strike terror into my heart.

It seems to be the area where all my lack of self-esteem is concentrated, even though regarding the art itself I feel I can rank up with the very good artists. There's just something about reaching out in front of other people and saying, "This is something that I really want, that really means a lot to me," that absolutely wreaks havoc upon the innermost parts of my self-confidence. I do it, but with the most God-awful stage fright. I become wooden and lose all my ability to sell myself. I am nasty to the people who are close to me. I become crushed if my attempts do not succeed.

One of the ideas I have had for a long time is to open my own gallery. Then I wouldn't have to go grovelling to gallery owners who have not the slightest interest in my work. I also would not have to split the selling price with the condescending bastards. There are some old houses in downtown Kingman that can be bought for around $35,000 to $60,000 that would make good galleries.

I have been doing some window shopping to see if it would be a good project to try here. The likelihood of my ever selling any paintings in Kingman seems to be the chance of a snowball in hell. However, tax-wise it makes sense. I also really love the old part of Kingman. It would give me a chance to try this in a very non-threatening place. There are no buyers, there is no Art World, there are only a few other artists in the area, although I feel that a lot of them might come to Kingman if word was passed around in various artists' communities.

I have been very active in talking to other artists and shop owners, business people and realtors about an artistic revitalization of downtown Kingman. You would laugh if you could see it. It's the sleepiest place I've been plunked down in for a long, long time, except maybe Twenty-Nine Palms. Boarded up, bombed-out buildings are somewhere in every block. Tumbleweed blows down the main street at noon...

In looking back over the last entry, I want to praise myself for completing the work for the slide registry. I also put my ad back in the little local paper. I gained two new students from the ad. Instead of carefully screening them, I am adopting the m.o. of "I'll take all comers" and see what happens. We're so damned broke. It's nice to have just a little pocket money. I also have been working in my Black Book where I put all my drawings, dreams and scraps of thought. It's OK. I like what I'm doing in my book. This is obviously one of my "incubation" periods I go through cyclically. I'm wondering what kind of paintings to show in Kingman... Smaller. Different. I've changed again and need time to absorb the change into my creative center, into my self.

October 3, 1989

I just came out of the studio with an absolute void. I feel kind of sick and empty, on edge. I keep waiting for something to come out, but nothing wants to. It's a lot like a being constipated. I want to say something, to push something out, but nothing comes. I don't know what to do with myself. I wander through the house looking for something to catch my interest.

I was supposed to have two students this afternoon, but one has pulled a no-show. When I spoke to her on the phone I didn't feel any curiosity or desire to work with her, so I am relieved in a way. I've just been saying yes to see what the universe might be sending my way. So the cosmic screening device seems to be in place and functioning.

I was looking in my Black Book at the drawing that I did last week when a student I like a lot was here. The drawing is of a woman out in the desert holding our missing cat. She is very deep, and so is the landscape. In fact I like it better than anything I've done in awhile. I do not know if I will make a painting of it or not. I like it, so that makes it a good candidate for an oil, but it seems like there is a re-charging phase going on — at least I hope that's what's happening. You never really believe it until it's ended and you are celebrating an upswing in the creative cycle.

Chapter 12

A WOMAN BEING TAKEN BY THE DESERT

My mother is dying . . . We plan a visit to Santa Fe . . .

October 8, 1989

A painting started coming out today, much to my surprise. I started work on a painting of the drawing I wrote about in the last entry. The picture has evolved from the original sketch; the woman is alone out in the desert merging with the yucca plants. She is melting into the desert shadows — or perhaps the shadows are merging to form the woman. There is a mystery about the painting that keeps me coming back to look at it, to daub paint here and there, smearing it with my middle right finger, wiping it off again.

I finally got out of the doldrums when Bob wanted to work on his writing on my work table, so I pulled my easel up next to him and put headphones on with Native American flute music. This seemed to help me get lost long enough to lay in most of the first layer of color. It all opened up after I listened in a very contemplative and drifting way for some time to the hypnotic music of Carlos Nakai, whose music really works for me. I floated for awhile on the sound. I thought about what the advantages might be to some peyote experimentation, if it would intensify my unconscious wilderness. Then I turned the painting upside-down and the whole thing went liquid. It shifted into a flowing river of shapes and colors.

I can't really consider taking peyote in the remotest way. When I took L.S.D. only one time I nearly lost my mind with my soul trailing after it like a banshee. With no chemicals at all I have managed to tear down quite a number of the walls between this world and the others. Sometimes material from my unconscious comes rushing up the pipes and I have very little defense against the backwash. Painting is plenty mind-expanding. It's also very grounding. It's a way to get with the Great Spirit, without the constant interference of the brain.

I'm getting ready to revisit my former life in Santa Fe. I haven't gone out into the desert for a paint. I don't care so much about that now that I have started on a painting. It will wait until I get back. I'm excited about going "home." I was willing to leave, but now I cannot wait to return — to see familiar and well-loved friends and places. I want to see adobe walls against the bluest sky. I want to wonder at the crosses out in the middle of nowhere, growing out of the red earth. I want to see New Mexico. I want to see the golden aspens in the mountains above Santa Fe once more.

I am suffering from a terrible case of homesickness. It has been nine months since my precipitous exit. I would like to go back to Santa Fe, where I used to get messages on my answering machine from my father. He might be looking for me there. We could talk like we used to and I could tell him about all the little things the baby is doing and saying now. I could get pregnant again and go on along the winding red dirt path and try to fill up the gaping holes that have been left in my heart and my soul and my life.

October 9, 1989

I am completely overcome by my feelings about our pending visit to Santa Fe. The most extraordinary pull to return there has been nagging at me day and night. Along with the pull is a most surprising "message" of the type I get from time to time. The message is that Santa Fe pulled me into its arms one time already to live there. If it wants me there again, it will pull me back again, against all odds and obstacles. And my hope is that that is exactly what will happen. I am full of longing to return to a place of beauty and natural spirituality.

It also came to me that if I can figure out how to load my old computer disc into this new computer, the story of how I was brought to Santa Fe in the first place would be there for me to read, in case I have forgotten how impossible and complex that passage of my life really was.

It is easy to forget the unbelievable power of surrender. In certain passages one feels abandoned by God — like somehow we have fallen out of favor with the universe, and will never feel contentment or fulfilled. No more miracles will come my way. I will have to settle for a life of mediocrity. For some of us an ordinary life would be worse than death! It is not that sometimes, in exhaustion from trying to keep my head above the waves in a sea of change, a little rest doesn't sound like the only thing that matters. It is not that I do not cry out to God to stop it, stop it, stop the onslaught of challenge and change. It is just that I also thrive on the pulsations, the eruptions, the agony and the ecstasy. Something in me becomes stronger every time I get pushed into the fire. All the extraneous bullshit is burned away, the excess baggage is torn from my claw-like hands. Relationships that hold me down are ripped away with no mercy and no anesthetic. All that is left is my heart, my soul, some loves, some painful memories, my painting. Very little else comes through. In the end I must say I am lucky to get through with even that much.

Perhaps that is what already has happened, and Kingman, Arizona is where I am supposed to be? It doesn't feel right, though. In the meantime I believe there are some things I can do here, even in Kingman, certain contributions which I can make. They are very small contributions, but the Universe does not seem to fault the size of what we give. It only seems to matter that I give what I am able, what I am asked to give. Anyway, it passes the time.

I looked at my painting I started yesterday, and had no desire to go near it. I didn't like it, in fact. It seemed to have gone dead on me. I have decided that if I do not want to complete paintings right now, I am not going to question that or try to force myself to go further. I am not going to sit here and try to make a decision, I am just going to watch myself and see what I do.

It's a path of growth I have found to be quite effective. I watch and let it unfold. Very out-of-control, as far as an intellectual locus of decision-forcing. What am I going to do? I don't know. And I am not interested in forcing myself to make decisions, goals, plans. Chaotic growth seems to be very compatible with the needs of my creative self, and it's what I intend to do about where I am and where I am going. Nothing. Be confused. Better shut off my head now and let the fog roll in.

October 17, 1989, Santa Fe

I woke up this morning all revved up, and eagerly got Sasha from her bed. I crashed through some barrier on the road to Santa Fe. It started something inside of me moving — something which has been stuck since I left.

We cried for hours in the car driving here. We saw many, many good and loving friends. We visited all the magical places that were so nurturing to us as individuals and as a couple. We went to Chimayo to eat the dirt. We lit candles and asked for a miracle along with the other people asking for miracles. We asked to be put where it is that we are supposed to be.

There's nothing like days and days of crying to get things in motion.

It took the death of my father and a sojourn in a lonely desert town to get me back to writing regularly in this record. It took a total uprooting to put me in such pain that I started to paint with determination for my sanity.

One of the effects of the overly quiet life in Kingman has been the reconnection to a creative current as strong as the one before I left L.A. Painting is the most pure connection I have to a spiritual source. When I left my life in Los Angeles, the shock was too great. It's rearranged my molecules. Now is a rime to re-collect all the threads left from the nuclear blast and begin weaving. I have never had time to absorb all the life changes that have happened to me since I met Bob.

Having a child is certainly the most profound experience I have had in my life so far, but integrating all the new and old parts of me has been a Herculean task. I have to work all the time to maintain my own center, particularly with a small person tugging at me. I am looking for myself, and I think I see her wandering out in the desert.

Another thread I dropped when I left my studio was the series on the tarot. I painted five cards of a possible twenty before the moving van rolled in. There are loose ends hanging there. It makes me angry and sad.

The moon was full two days ago. It's a better time to complete projects than to start new ones. I have a painting on my easel I can work on. It's not holding my interest right now. In some ways it is easier to drag myself back to it though, rather than carve a new path through the jungle. Someone's coming for a lesson today. Life goes on in Kingman. I quietly wait for the spaceships to arrive and take me back to New Mexico.

October 19, 1989

Just finished a letter to my friend, Nancy Sandstrom, in New York. Even though I have very little time to write them, letters give me a chance to clarify things which are churning inside of me. I was talking to her about the feelings I have about wanting to return to New Mexico, specifically about well-meaning friends who start chiming in with a chorus of opinions, i.e.: This is where you are supposed to be, or "It's God's will." Is God writing them memos, or something?

When I'm tuned into myself and hooked up to the god-force I intuitively know what's right for me. I also know what doesn't feel right. I believe these "feelings" actually come from God. I don't go out go out and force these things to happen. Instead, I open up my mind to all possibilities and cooperate. We all deserve the chance to follow our dream, and the dignity of living with our choices. As I go along further in my life I have come to doubt the existence of mistakes. I may have a lot of bruises, but they are learning bruises.

Over the last few years I suffered an enormous amount of remorse after leaving Philippe. I do not feel that the way I left him was kind or even "right." I know that it brought out strength and ingenuity in me that I never would have summoned in my comfortable life. Also, my leaving revealed hidden parts of his character I never would have seen as long as he was calling the shots and getting his own way. As I said, there's nothing quite so revealing as saying no to someone. He was not the kind of person for me to have as a long-term partner. Ethical differences — on both sides.

Anyway what came to me as I was mulling over the question of here or there or everywhere was this: I will never know, I will never really live until I get up out of my spectator's armchair and quit using the remote control. I have to try it all, sometimes back and forth, back and forth. Some risks pay off better than others.

I get put off by the way people around me constantly are putting their fearful input in as soon as my edges start blurring. Friends often get scared when they sense massive changes — they might be left behind in the wreckage. Much dumb advice comes, unasked for. It leaves me more and more alone with each cycle of change. I get angry about this, but that's an improvement. I used to think they must be right.

October 29, 1989

As I began to write this evening I checked the date. I realized that it the anniversary of my sister's death, one day after her birthday. She died the day after she turned 37. It is the first year I haven't gotten very, very depressed. It all just kind of went by in a quiet parade. It took a lot of crying to get here. I miss her. I especially miss her warped sense of humor.

Yesterday I was thinking about the indignity of the way my father died, slack-jawed, drooling and bellowing like a long-time inmate at a nuthouse. I thought of all the letters I have written and conversations or confrontations in my life. Death is so terribly cruel a lover, and no amount of pleading, therapy, negotiation, rage, or just plain whining is going to change the end even one tiny bit. It is the Great Unnegotiable. There is no one to complain to about it. Nothing will change the ugliness, the degradation. Undoubtedly this sordidness is what is in back of many of the melodramatic religious sacraments conjured up like a smoke screen to cover up the reality from those who cannot look into the uncaring maw of death. "He is saved!" Yes, but he is dying. "Life everlasting!" But she is dead.

This last week I spent a lot of time crying and digging, pulling and prying, to dislodge the unexpressed feelings that have been keeping me from painting.

I uncovered a tremendous amount of anger — a lot of it towards my mother for making me into the little emotional time bomb that I am. I feel like the Lawrence Harvey character in *The Manchurian Candidate*. It's clear to me that when I was a little pip-squeak in my drunken home growing up, bailing Mom and Dad out of various jails, making the rounds of hospitals after fights, accidents, drunken "heart attacks," various and sundry false alarms, I was fully brainwashed into abject co-dependency. When the red queen dropped on the table, I could do nothing to stop myself — I had to go take care of her and the mountain of shit she was dragging around with her.

Now some of that being-there-for-others stuff is okay with me. I would think I was a real jerk for not coming, comforting, loving, but I am so angry it is impossible for me to locate any love I might have for my mom at this time. People who are merely in their first decade of therapy can wisely say "Oh but who are you really angry with? It's you. You're mad at yourself for allowing this to happen." Wrong. I am furious at my all-American Mom for making me this way without my permission or knowledge when I was a little, tiny girl so that when push came to shove, I would drop my own life to come and take care of her. I am lucky I have a life left.

The upshot of this long drawn out diatribe is that as soon as the anger started to surface I wanted to paint. I have been able to work through the painting where I got stuck weeks ago. It was impossible for me to resolve this stubborn painting until I could just get really pissed off. In fact, I've been getting pissed off all over the place. It's hard to paint when you are busy holding down the lid on an over-full garbage can.

The good thing about not wanting to work, finding myself unable to go on in the middle of a painting, is that it let me know that something was out of balance inside of me. Nothing was going to flow until I took the time to sit down with the angry child inside of me and find out what was bugging her. She needed to be noticed. She needed some comforting. Even with many years of therapy and twelve-step groups, the healing is slow.

November 15, 1989

Started to feel better about my work. I'm still banging away at the painting, "A Woman Being Taken by the Desert." She's been a very, very difficult birth. I've hit on a few ideas about why she's giving me such a hard time.

One is that I live in an Art Vacuum. This is a community where few people give a shit about art. Maybe six people see my work in the course of a week. Many of the rewards of art come from having others enjoy it. It's the difference between having sex with a responsive partner or just doing yourself. I need some kind of exchange of my art with other people. My paintings are still hanging in the bank in downtown Kingman, but I hear very little feedback about it.

Then, I have plenty of work to do after the death of my father. Not all of it is going to be on canvas. New tangles and resolutions demand much of my attention. I'm still doing major excavations in the ruins. I can't build a new life until I clear off my building site. A good foundation is needed.

Bob and I were talking today about how hard it sometimes is to put his writing first, with a thousand other parts of life competing for his attention. When I started out, all my teachers were artists. By their example over many years, it seemed more natural to put painting first. It's very hard for a woman with a family to give herself permission to put her creative life first. A regular job — of course! I still feel the needs of everyone around me, but I know that if I stay at my work table long enough, someone else will step over to the stove and feed the hungry. I know when I'm trying to work, the best thing is to not make

WARRIOR WOMAN
1990, oil 4′ x 6′

MADONNA I
1987, oil, 18″ x 24″

DREAM ABOUT THE MOTHER
1987, oil, 18″ x 24″
from the collection of
Mr. & Mrs. William Rossiter
Santa Fe, New Mexico

DIA DE LOS MUERTOS
1990, oil, 48'' x 48''

THE PATH
1990, oil, 4' x 6'
from the collection of
Mr. & Mrs. David Montgomery
Kingman, Arizona

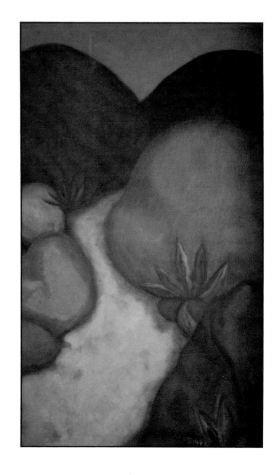

FUNERAL OF THE ARTIST
1986, oil, 5′ x 7′

FRIENDS
1986, oil, 5′ x 6′

THE SACRED DREAM
1990, oil, 6' x 12'

THE SECRET PLACE
1990, oil, 24" x 30"

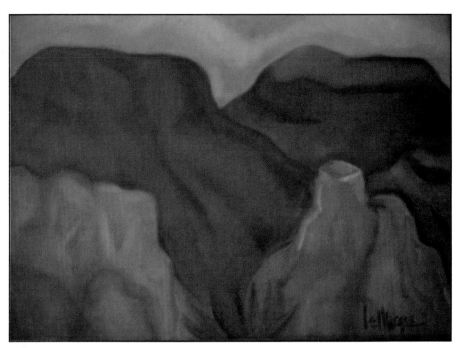

KINGMAN MESAS
1990, oil, 18″ x 24″

GHOST DANCERS
1990, oil, 6′ x 8′

SELF PORTRAIT PREGNANT
1987, oil, 30″ x 40″

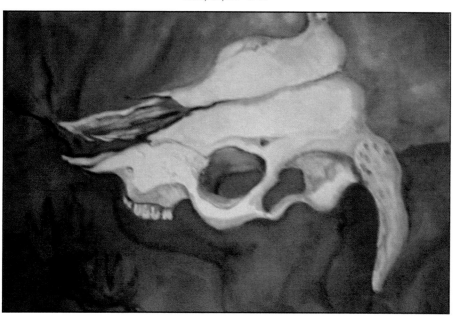

SKULL WITH CHAMISA
1987, oil, 24″ x 30″

BLACK OGRE
1990, oil, 4' x 6'

the bed. In fact, I frequently don't get out of my nightgown when I'm on a painting binge.

My art is the channel to the most pure, essential part of me. I am not totally my feelings. I am not my inner child, although the child inside of me is an essential part of my creativity. I am not my marriage, although it provides a terrific framework for growth. I am an artist. When I am doing my art I am hooked up to the Great Spirit and all is well with me. Ultimately, putting myself and my art first is the best for all the people that I love. If not, then I must re-examine the choices I have made in the people I surround myself with. I don't allow myself to be mutilated.

Back to the "Woman Who Is Being Taken by the Desert." She is a haunting vision, melting out in the late afternoon shadows. She is about the experience of cutting away to find the essence of myself, the strong core necessary to sustain me through the next leg of the journey — which I sense is coming to another turning point. Everything which is not essential will be cast to one side. Ripped away, if my memories of past transitions is any indication. That is how this woman came to be standing alone out in the Wasteland. The Corridor. She is gathering strength through her cold, bare feet from the earth, our mother. She is being pushed by the wind. We all are familiar with the winds of change — bend or break, move or be torn from the earth. The mesas, the pyramids of the American desert, are stabilizing the landscape, the woman. It has been much harder for me to find her this time, to talk to her, to visualize her. I do not think she wanted to come out into the open, but I can coax her out with love, patience, attention to myself. It has taken days. It has taken weeks. It has taken months, and years, stretching all the way back into other lives, stretching into a stellar future far past ordinary vision. But I've got time.

Chapter 13

VISIONS OF CHANGE

Sun dogs . . . "El Angel de Santa Fe" . . . Solstice—I light a candle in the darkness . . .
House for sale . . . More anger . . .

November 22, 1989

Today I saw two Sun Dogs in the sky, a special occasion. I have visions of
great change.

I have been working on a painting from a drawing in my sketch book which
I did after a pretty dry period, inspiration-wise. The image came to me in Santa
Fe, and I decided to use it during the planetary time-warp that took place last
weekend.

In the painting there is a woman standing holding a sleeping child in her
arms at night. In back of her, protecting her, engulfing her, is "El Angel de Santa
Fe." He is deep violet, visible to her third eye, and radiant. He is gently guiding
her and bringing her back home. He is lending her his strength to make a
difficult journey back to a place that will nurture her and her family. There are
some adobe buildings at the foot of the Sangre de Cristos. Her man is waiting
for her there, along with their future.

This vision was profoundly affecting to me at the time it first appeared. Now
that I am here I am using the technique of visualization as a transformative tool.
That is where I want to be, working, loving, and growing.

Students have been appearing so I've been painting regularly. Magic
happens for me when I am painting and letting the creative energy come right
on through, out into the room for others to use as well. I work whenever they
come for lessons. I show my two kid students my paintings... "Oh those things?
They're dead bodies."... Their open minds soak it all in. They would never have
access to a person like me under the everyday circumstances of their lives. It
really tickles me. They show me their pocket knives and tell me about their little
sisters. They bring me pictures of their pets. They are a joy to me. We paint
together and I wonder about the impact that my presence, my words, my
attitudes are going to have on them after I am gone. I choose my words carefully.

I still use many, many things that Dorothy Royer taught me when I was a
kid of five painting with her in her workshop in West Hollywood — don't use
erasers, quit painting that same old rose you always paint. Try to paint
something new in a different way. What a teacher! I tracked her down thirteen
years later in my quest to find my path. I remembered her. She was radiant with

an inner light. She gave me strength. She became a pivotal figure in my life, opening up doors I had never even heard of in buildings I had seen in dreams. Teaching art is definitely a special assignment.

December 21, 1989

According to the spirits I celebrate with, today is winter solstice. I lit a candle last night in front of a pile of bones and thought about the last year, as I will continue to do today. I thought of all the death that came crashing down around us in the first months of 1989. I thought about my brother re-entering my life. I thought about my cousin Michael who has AIDS and the powerful letter that he sent. I thought about all the beautiful paintings I have done this year, this painful, painful year that ends and begins today. We have survived and not only that. We have evolved. All the painting and writing I have done here are a direct response to death and transformation.

The death of my father and the ensuing feelings have forced me to re-explore the areas of anger and the damage that was done to me without my choice or consent. Although my parents supported me totally in my art, the effects of years of drinking and violence have undermined me at every turn, including my ability to reach the next level of artistic success. I am always "less than." I am always "unworthy." Each time I reach for fulfillment, my hand shakes a little.

Several months ago I had a dream about asking a woman who lives here in Kingman to work with me as a therapist. She is a psychiatric nurse. It was an extraordinary dream full of rich images — the removal of beautiful masks of leaves and seashells. Since that time we have been climbing down into the catacombs of my childhood one more time. There is a sea of broken glass between me and me. I must do more housecleaning, sweeping out the dust, throwing out what is no longer useful. Every few years I re-begin this process that began with my first therapist in 1969. In amongst the towering mounds of trash I see little diamonds glittering like beacons in the darkness.

When I sit down to work now there is an outpouring of angry images. I am yelling at my mother, my father. I am reaching into my lungs and pulling out a hard black stone of sickness and tension. I throw it back at my mother. "You can have this back. It wasn't mine in the first place."

I think about how I started out my life so sick with a severe case of asthma, surrounded by smoking, drunken, fighting adults. When I heard about hell in the Catholic school I attended, I knew I wouldn't have to go there. I was already living in hell. I was doing enough penance for a future lifetime of sin. This came to me at around the age of six. What a start!

I felt defective and weak. I was the only one in my family to get (need) extensive therapy. For fourteen years I was the only one who admitted to a drug and alcohol problem. I got sober and clean at age twenty-three. My doctor told me I was showing signs of emphysema in my chest x-ray. After quitting a four pack a day cigarette habit fifteen years ago, my lung problems have all but disappeared. My sister died of cancer at age thirty-seven. It was in her lungs as well as every place else. My father had emphysema. My mother has emphysema now. I was able to jump off the speeding train before it went off the cliff. I'm clean and sober and growing. Therapy pays. Believe it. Don't wait until after the x-rays.

There's no way to circumvent the feelings and memories that my unconscious is processing at this time. No "pretty" pictures, can emerge past the parade of grotesqueries. I am full of rage, by design, for my survival. That is what I am painting, drawing and dreaming these days. It's what I want to let die with the dying light of this last year. Art is the primary tool I use for my exorcism.

My sick parents made that lifesaving tool available to me. Ironic, isn't it? It's hard for people to understand when I tell them what incredible parents I was given, but it's the art that makes me say it. They nearly destroyed me in the acid bath of their alcoholism, but they threw me a very spiritual life jacket at the same time — a tool of true transformation. Art, and the wise ones who taught it to me, kept me alive until I could get help, do therapy, and find the various twelve step programs. This in turn kept me alive so I could fulfill my assignment in this life — to live the life of an artist, and let others know that they too can do this.

January 1, 1989

Today was a day full of talking and thinking about the creative process. Bob and I decided to have an A.R.T.S. meeting in Voyager II. We were careening home across the desert after a Fellini-esque New Year's Eve in Las Vegas. I never thought in a million years or even in other lives that I would look forward so to going to Las Vegas. Gives you some idea what Kingman is like.

We talked about how creative people will often go to any length to avoid doing their art. Some like to eat cookies, some go shopping, some masturbate. We will do anything to avoid doing the thing which makes us feel better than anything else in the world. The trick I learned when I was about to go out shopping one day was to turn around and go back into the studio and paint. It was as if I had accidentally thrown a bridle on a wild horse. What a ride! It was great and a hell of a lot cheaper. I began to get a handle on why it was I just didn't seem to have enough energy or drive to paint. I was afraid of the wild stallion in my studio.

Creative energy is frightening to those who don't have it. It is far more frightening to those of us who do. So we get rid of it any other way we can think of. We talk compulsively on the telephone, thereby discharging the extra voltage and spending the need to communicate from the most raw parts of ourselves. We fix other people's lives. We run errands overly efficiently. When we come home we drop from exhaustion. "You don't expect me to paint (write, play the piano, go dancing, etc.)!"

Another trick we like to play is "Postponement." It has many variations, but the one I hear most often is "I'll start this great new routine tomorrow." I mean, if you want to create, do it NOW. DO IT NOW. Put your book down, hang up the phone, cancel your luncheon date. Do it right now. If you're at work, when you leave to go home for dinner pick up a sandwich at the deli. Do not turn on the great Passivity Machine — hold your sandwich in your dominant hand and paint with the other. Write holding the baby who is grabbing the computer and the paper clips. Plunk her on your lap, attach her to your tit. Start a dance class with your friends and their two-year-olds this week. Hire African drummers to come bang the drums until your hips and feet can't hold still any more.

I bought a huge, flat Tarahumara drum. "I can't play the drums." I bought a small drum for Sasha. Every so often we get our drums out and march through the house out into the desert pounding, reverberating, stepping to the memories of other places, other times. These things must be done at the moment when there is even the slightest desire flickering by. Start quickly, before the descent of the Valkyries, the ones who are so good at telling you why it is that you can't do it. Stand up and DANCE. Don't go home and think about how you'll do it next time, because every time we do that the little voice gets less sure of itself, harder to hear. Eventually it is drowned out by the bustle of everyday life, only to be heard in the brief moments when we sit down quietly with nothing to do.

Many lives have gone from start to finish never being touched by the creative river. We must sit down at the computer. Without waiting for the right time we must step up onto the stage and act. When it wakes you up on nights when the moon is full, get up and do it. Go to your straight job tired, and with bloodshot eyes, because creativity is the force that can make a key to swing the door of your little prison open wide. Pick up the key right now. Let your family shake their heads and call you a dreamer — an idiot, perhaps. They will walk on in their grey business suits and you will stay behind and build castles out of driftwood on the beach...

January 13, 1990

It's 11:15 p.m. in Kingman. At this hour of the night I have time for myself. Following my own advice to give in to the slightest urge to do something creative, here I am.

91

WARRIOR WOMAN

Yesterday I brought my disintegrating mother home from the hospital I knew she would never come home from. She takes 22 pills every day, and numerous breathing treatments, hooked up to all manner of throbbing machines. Her pulse must be checked first thing every morning before some of the medication can be taken.

All of this was casually tossed into my reluctant hands at the hospital. I don't feel like painting much right now. I just want to run away. But I'll paint whenever I can drag myself to it — without it I am center-less. My world would be reduced to the world of the caretaker — the one who lives for others. Didi is coughing now... I'll go check and come back.

Yes, well, back to work. The strong and stubborn heart of my mother beats on.

It's really hard. I hate it. I'm not this unselfish. I'll paint about it. I wish I had someone to paint it with. I do have one student who is a possibility — the woman I trade therapy for painting lessons with. Anyway, I'm angry. I spent a wretched childhood centered around her and my dad's drinking. Now my life is centered around her illness — which is probably brought on by a lifetime of alcohol and cigarettes.

I went to a little gathering of people interested in "metaphysics" today. Ohmygod. Well, it was a good afternoon's entertainment except for a couple of incredibly sick cookies from Southgate, California — snake oil salesmen, reading auras and so forth. They did not make the mistake of tampering with mine. Many of the guests were preparing for the arrival of spacecraft.

I had a surprise chat with one of the guests there. It seems she knows one of my students very well. She told me with self-importance about how she "pokes fun at" the girl's work. She points out the flaws for her. The child is ten-years-old. It gave me a terrible feeling of suffocation, anger and despair when I heard this. I thought of how many supposedly well-meaning boobs have crushed people who were tentatively opening to their creativity. I said many pointed things to her, that she was way out of line criticizing a child's artistic efforts, but in her righteousness she couldn't grasp a word of what I was saying.

The pain that I felt after this encounter was terrible. I had a vision of this very destructive force around this beautiful, imaginative child, this hard old woman crushing her confidence in the guise of telling the truth, or helping her, or toughening her up for the world. I know she loves this little girl. It was like the horror I felt when I took the alcoholism counseling course and realized how unbelievably sick, self-important, and of course psychopathically right many of the people who were taking, as well as teaching, the course were. I figure the critic will read this book one day, but I think she will be so sure that what she did was right that she will know that these are obviously just the ravings of another disturbed person. But I could have strangled her with her rolled down stockings just the same.

However, the upshot of this is that I have armed this bright, shining little girl-artist with a few grenades for Mildred. I told her many people will project all of their own weaknesses, fears of experimentation, and incredible inadequacies and even jealousies onto an artist's work, i.e. "The Critics' Syndrome," so well known to the artist — the cutting words, dripping in false sweetness, from someone who cannot do art themselves.

Sometimes one will encounter this in a different form — the "Gallery Owners' Syndrome." Some gallery owners love to tell artists how to work because they are not creating themselves. In Hollywood, writers continually run into this when called in to pitch a story, or revise scripts so that those who are utterly unable to produce a finished script on their own can manage to "save the show." Sometimes it's your nextdoor neighbor or your mother who is doing this, and we must all learn at last to stop showing unsupportive people our precious work. Should they manage to find something we have made — and they will find it, no matter where you have hidden it — the besieged artiste should concentrate on her critic's flaws — i.e.: their shitty choice of nylon dress socks with their madras bermudas or their fluorescent blue eye shadow, in order to keep perspective on who is really trying to dictate our aesthetic standards. When you're strong enough, tell them you don't want to hear what they have to say. Turn your back on them when they are mid-precious-sentence and fart.

January 17, 1990

I've been reading back over the first part of this journal. It's pretty hard to swallow yourself, sometimes.

There is a powerfully transformative tool in an honest record of who I am and where I have been. Upon re-reading it several times, the patterns are etched out starkly. Rewriting, re-reading, rewriting yet again, nausea threatens. I read it and see that I am reaching yet another turn in the spiral of my learning. Another tidal wave is moving towards my life. Inside, my animal self keeps warning me — something's coming, something's changing, get ready. I wonder how much is going to be lost this time, who's going to get splattered in the blast. I'm scared. I'm really scared, but there is nothing I can do about it. It's the next turn of the wheel of life.

I'm still painting, haltingly. Bob and Sasha and I are on the red road. There is a lone figure walking a long way down the path. Someone still farther along is waiting for her. It is my mother and my father. He is waiting for her to join him. The image in paint is disturbing and transforming. My mom doesn't come out of her room much anymore, so I don't have to worry about her seeing it. This world is going to be a sadder and lonelier place without her. I am in terrible pain from waiting for it all to happen so I can go on with my life. She looks like she's dying, she returns from the edge of death again and again. She bounces back, but I'm am not bouncing back so well anymore.

Back when I first started this book it was coming out so hot and heavy I thought it would take no time at all to complete it. I had no idea of the enormity of the changes that were about to happen to me. It seems like a gigantic, unfinishable task right now. Sort of like going into the delivery room and suddenly realizing how much it is actually going to hurt, and the process can't be stopped. The painkillers don't work like you'd counted on them working, and there's no way to stop the labor.

Since I started this thing I've been through divorce, breakups of relationships, forcibly leaving the city and all my friends I'd loved for years. I have survived and flowered following a life-and-death struggle to not fall in love, ensuing pregnancy, birth, marriage. I have experienced death three times in this brief space of time, with another one in-process. I went away for a weekend and never went back home to Santa Fe again. No wonder it's been so hard to keep writing and painting.

It's been a vivid life.

March 13, 1990

It's been awhile since I have had anything to say here, and it is an odd sensation as I sit down to the computer, feeling around for the foot pedal — oh yeah! That's the sewing machine! How do I make my fingers remember how to make the words come out?

Also funny — my mate is writing again, and suddenly I feel like working too. It is a power plant, two creative people living under the same roof. Also, my mom's health is good right now. The pressure is off, leaving me more open, with space and time to observe and comment. Anyway, Bob's asleep, the moon is full, and I had to get up and write. It's the right time. It's my own time.

We have put the Kingman house on the market. Even though we all love the land, everyone in the clan seems to be pretty much drying up and dying here, so it's time to look for a new cave. I have found the lack of an art world here to be unbearable. I really miss having an outlet for my own work, besides the few people I can coerce into coming here to see my paintings. I also am feeling the incredible dearth of other people's art for me to see. It's a stagnant little pond here, and I want to be part of the world of creativity once again. I have been able to produce plenty of my own work in Kingman, but it's not enough to do it just for me.

I have greatly enjoyed the contact with the students I have had here. There's Sharon, with whom I trade painting lessons for therapy. She has a wonderful succession of images that just come marching out of her sub-conscious unimpeded. In turn I go to her house and beat up her furniture, frighten her cats, and throw up with her holding my head. Afterwards I fold up and crawl into her arms and listen to her heart beat. It's a good working relationship.

I also teach a wonderful young boy of twelve who beats himself up, mercilessly criticizing himself and his art with the viciousness of an adult. I am so glad to see him painting though. His father's well-meaning answer to his lack of self-confidence is more sports. His mother, however keeps bringing him back to the creative path. It is very hard for him, and hard for me to see such a young person already nearly crippled by his own self-criticism. So little of what I say seems to give him hope. I say the stuff to him anyway, about what a good artist he is, but I see little belief on his part. This one is hard for me.

My third student is Shelby, a girl of ten. I have written about her before. Now she is going to be very hard to leave. I called her mother to let her know we were going to put the house up for sale. I remembered how crushed I was when Serisawa left Los Angeles, and thought I should let her get used to the idea before she saw the for sale sign up in front of the place. I know she spent the night crying, as I did when I knew I was going to lose this very magical teacher from my own life.

I told her that when she gets old enough, when her mother thinks she is ready, she can come and be with me for a week or two. We can paint together and I can take her out to galleries and museums. Sounds terrific, doesn't it? To me, too. And then this very special relationship can be allowed to continue for both of us.

There are many strange and interesting types of people hiding in the bushes and mobile homes of Kingman. Take Ed and Stacy Toten, for instance... a gifted channeler and his equally gifted wife. For the last few weeks we have been visiting them to watch him do his explorations and pass on pertinent messages from our respective spirit guides.

My current guide and teacher is Yetna, a beloved woman from a local Native American tribe. I asked her if I once was her, but she said, no, we were simply in the same tribe. At that time I was a young girl there, in her clan, and she had chosen to teach me as her successor in healing and the mysteries of life. In fact it was she who got me up out of bed to come in here and write.

When Ed was channeling her, I asked her what she could tell me about my work. She said I must paint what I love. I would be helped by a period of meditation before painting. I have never been more affected by the work of another psychic as I have been by the few contacts we have had with this couple.

A great, stifling cloud has been lifted off of me, Bob, our family. We needed assistance from the spirits in a different way, and the healing results of this particular contact have been dramatic and unexpected.

Many of my images originate in visions. I intend to explore this source, see if I can voluntarily stimulate it at this time. It is the week before vernal equinox — a potent time for creativity. The desert is throbbing with blood, life, birth. Sometimes I really love it here in Kingman. I do not want to leave the desert yet. Maybe never. There is nothing in the universe quite like spring in the desert. It pounds in your blood and tingles in your fingers. I have to work to discharge the energy from my hands.

Chapter 14

THE SACRED DREAM

Spring Equinox . . . The story of Diana the Huntress . . .
The Path—a change in direction . . .

March 20, 1990

Today was the first day of spring. I went out into the desert with a willow wreath on my head. I took one for my friend Laurel, who is always with me in a disembodied form. I lit some cedar incense and shook my willow buds over the ground.

Guided by a dream, I buried a small clay Mother Goddess figure in the sand. I turned my hands towards each other until I could feel them vibrating. I turned them towards my face to direct some of this energy towards myself, for strength and healing. I turned my hands back towards each other, to pump up my creativity. Lastly, I turned my hands towards the earth and directed all my healing abilities into the Mother.

In order to feel the power of the desert, I took off my shoes. In a squatting position I put both hands down on the warm ground. I took in energy through my feet and pushed it back out through my hands. I sang a song with no words. The earth felt warm and alive pulsating under my hands and feet.

I had a very significant dream several nights ago, in Desert Hot Springs. Things generally get very stirred up for me there. I dreamed I was looking down at a newspaper. On the cover was a color photograph of a tribe of American Indians all decked out in the most extraordinary Kachina garb, as it would look after being filtered through my sub-conscious. After seeing them all looking out at me, seeming to be communicating something very important, I moved to an opening in a nearby rock formation.

As I approached the stone, I knew it was one of the ancient power sites. It didn't look terribly special, but I knew power could be accessed easily there. There was some pecking on the rock and many, many footprints in the sand. I pulled the formation open wide enough to allow several people to enter the small cave. I summoned three other people, including my husband, my mother, and one unidentified person. I instructed them as I was being directed by the tribe to turn their hands down towards the earth, directing all of their healing abilities and thoughts down into the core of the planet.

As we did this, the earth began to tremble slightly. Shortly I felt a need to emerge from this earthen womb through an opening in a voluminous, blue, tent-like piece of fabric. I continued to direct my power down into the ground as I walked over to pond and sat down on the banks. The ground was steadily rolling harder and harder. I called the others to my side at the water. It was a violent earthquake by this time.

My mother was the slowest and the last to come. As she approached, she jumped into the pond in fear. I spoke these words to the others as I pulled her out by one hand which I had hold of: "She's jumped in the water because she thinks the earth did not want our offering, but that is not the case. She is rolling and bucking as she accepts our gift into her great body. She is well pleased, and it means that our power has been received and stored." Later I saw my mother in the arms of a male friend who was trying to make sense of it all for her.

When I went back into the dream, the tribe members told me they had sent me a Sacred Dream. They told me I came from them long ago, and they were trying to pass on the things that they had learned. I plan on beginning a large painting of them when I get back from New York.

March 27, 1990

New York! New York, New Jersey, Pennsylvania... I loved it. I've never been east, other than a quick touchdown to go some place else. I really loved it — the contrasts between the different locations. We went to New Hope, Pennsylvania, and I wanted to move right in. It was just the kind of artists' colony I fantasize about living in. We went to the Met, where I was able to eat some paintings as well as a civilized lunch, gawking at New Yorkers.

When we got home, I pushed myself to open one of the giant crates I keep my future museum pieces in. It's been a long time since I worked on a big one. I chose a 6' x 5' blank and put it on the easel to look at the whiteness, its vacantness, for awhile. I put my preliminary sketch up on the wall to glance at it. It struck me how much more impact the piece would have if I did it in two panels of that same size. So that's how I've laid it out.

There isn't anything in the world like the effect of painting an image life-size, especially if the vision comes from your dreams (What's life-size in your dreams?). The tribe is taking on life. They are poised, breathing steadily, gazing at me. They are ready to get up and dance again. There is a feeling of really Standing on the Edge, as the characters begin to take form. This painting has formed an unobstructed channel between my conscious self and the depths of my being. I am listening. I am looking. I am present. I usually work in fairly short, intense bursts when I paint so large. There is a crafty madness that overtakes me if I go on too long at a time. It is as if the unconscious has slipped through a crack in the wall.

My student, Shelby, was here when I started the piece. It is a rich thing to see the wonder in her eyes as she watches the magic come out of the paintbrush. It makes the painting all the more fun for me.

I want to have a gallery/studio open to the public. People should be able to watch as artists work. It gives them the visual experience that human beings are capable of giving form to anything that they can possibly imagine. People should make art. People should be able to come into the studio and watch art being made. It brings about a slow but unavoidable transformation. We become ourselves at last. First in the studio, then out in the world.

When we were in New York we were with a group of people who have recently written books in the self-help, co-dependency field. Three people at the table where I was sitting had published books. Others drifted by during the evening. It is a vision quest to sit down and attempt to write something like this with no publisher, no financial backing, no agent, no publicist and worst of all, no confidence.

I spent a good part of the evening comparing my squirmy insides to their polished (sort-of) outsides. The only thing that keeps me going sometimes is that I know my art reaches inside of people. That is a gift that was given to me freely and comes to me unblocked. Not only can I paint and express myself in all sorts of varied art techniques, I am a writer. I still have to keep my material moving out into the world to keep the creative drive flowing freely from its source.

Nevertheless, the desire to get under the table gets pretty strong when I think about how the hell I am actually going to do this. Cocktail party atmospheres are a perfect place to indulge in this type of self-flagellation. I haven't exactly been a success in the gallery scene. Not many people give a shit about me or my art in the big A.W. (Art World). This also seems like one of the key reasons I want to put this material out there. If I, a little golden worm, can do this, so can you. But at some point I am really going to have to stick my neck out with this very personal and revealing manuscript. It's hard to take rejection when the material is so tied up with my puny self and fragile ego. Arrgh. I am a little whining golden worm.

March 30, 1990

This is a story I told for my friend/therapist today. On the way in my little interior Nazi told me I should stop in the laundry room and do some wash, maybe fold a few things. If a creative person ever wishes to accomplish anything other than domestic excellence, it is imperative to ignore the sirens and tie oneself to the nearest easel, art class, or dance performance. The story went like this:

Diana the Huntress was walking in an oak forest close to the end of day. She was accompanied by her wolf dog, and carried a bow. The oak trees were dense, and the light was mauve. She sat down in a circle of oaks to be re-centered in her instincts. In this way she would sense when game was near, and she was hungry.

The birds were singing and she listened with every part of her being to their voices. Her spirit soared upward as she followed their lilting and varied song. Suddenly all was silent, and she knew that a stag was approaching her. She raised her bow and shot an arrow that sank deep into the breast of the stag. He did not fall as she approached to thank him for giving his life to feed her and her faithful wolf dog.

"Forgive me, oh great and noble dweller of the forest, for taking your life on this evening. Thank you for giving your life that my life may go on." Before she could continue, the great stag spoke, "Little sister, today is not the last day of my life. It is a very different sort of arrow that would spill my life's blood on this leafy earth. I am here to speak to you of certain things which you must do, else your own arrows might turn back upon you and bring about your downfall. Death is not an option for the Immortals, but there are far worse fates than death."

"Well, what is it that you wish to tell me?," said Diana as her dog wind-scented the stag from a respectful distance.

"First, you must sit down upon the earth, your mother, and let her energy flow up into you. You must let her heal you. You must become exactly like a stone: heavy and grounded."

"I know this already. Why are you telling me this as if I were a child?"

"Because you never take the time to do it anymore," he said with a voice rich and slow.

"Is there more?" she asked.

"You must push everything else out of your mind and focus up high, on the star which gives direction to your journey. It is the only way you will be strong enough and focussed enough to reach your destination, your heart's desire."

"I am a goddess! Why do you presume to teach me anything? There is nothing I do not know! There is no secret unknown to me."

"I am here to tell you this because you are so very busy being a goddess, and you do not make the time anymore to do these things for yourself. I repeat: make yourself like a stone on the earth and focus on the star."

With the snap of a twig the spell was broken. The stag crashed back into the undergrowth and scrambled up an impossible incline. On the ground where he had stood lay a golden arrow. Diana picked it up with a small laugh and placed it in the quiver on her back. She patted her wolf dog on the head. "Nothing to eat for our supper, but much food for thought. Come my trusted friend, let us sit here under the twisty boughs and be like two rocks." The moon rose huge and golden over the canyon.

April 16, 1990

The 'for sale' sign is in front of the house and I await a new assignment.

I'm still working slowly, savoring the big kachina painting. One of the issues I have been struggling with the last few months is the awareness of my age. I'll be 39 this year, and while I am not so stupid as to think that that is old, I also know that I am a far cry from the eighteen-year-old ideal woman of the American Dream. Aging is a condition which is known to be irreversible at this time. It makes me feel very strange and sad to know that I am losing value in the shallow society I live in, instead of gaining in stature as women do in the oriental cultures, the Native American tribes. It is a painful realization that there is really nothing I can do about it except avoid people who live by these values, avoid watching advertisements and most programs on TV, and keep painting.

I have been bringing up the issue of aging with every woman I am close to, to gain some kind of insight and knowledge. There are very few appealing role models for this process, although the art world holds a certain regard for the accomplishments of many years in the arts. As I was working on my Sacred Dream painting, I was moved to paint the hair of one of the dancing figures silver. The moment my brush touched the canvas I knew that something very meaningful was being given to me by my unconscious: the image of my Beloved Woman came to life in this world, radiant and full of power, before my unbelieving eyes. I felt the strength move through her outstretched bird wings and up my brush. I knew she was there to instruct me and protect me. She told me not to lose heart. My greatest value in this life is not in my beauty. I am to be a beacon to other women. I am an example to others of the true beauty of women — which is within, not on the surface. This beauty does not fade with the passage of years, but grows stronger with learning and the various experiences of life.

Tonight I went to a meeting. I needed to talk about some very painful and intimate things. A woman who detests me came into the room with her man-pet. After I speak she always manages to share about what I have said in an extremely veiled but vicious way. It isn't just me she does this to, but anyone who speaks freely or openly. Just before my turn to talk I felt my Beloved Woman stretch out her wings behind me. The woman fled the room. Her pet slunk after her.

Yesterday my pal Susan & Sasha & I went out for a hike in the desert. I had the baby in my backpack when she suddenly looked up and said "Rainbow!" I looked up to see something I have never seen before. We were in a shifting power vortex — the clouds were being sucked up as if through a funnel right over our heads. I began reeling with a sensation something like an elevator dropping out from under your feet. Whatever was happening with the clouds out in the desert was incomprehensible to my rational mind. The feeling was one of being sucked up with the clouds as they moved in this unnaturally fast and dizzying fashion.

What was it we saw? I don't know. It was an opening of some kind, a sucking force of expansion and movement. I let the top of my head open up and the insides of my being were pulled up with the clouds for just a few moments before my mind interfered with its fearfully analytical chatter. We knew something special had happened. As we walked further we came upon numerous indigo flowers. I did not recognize the leaves right away because they are so different in California where I first ranged into the hills gathering herbs, but the flowers were the unmistakably stacked flowers of sage. Susan and I gathered handfuls of sage and stuffed them into the baby backpack. The Kingman wind was whipping around us savagely. The scent of sage wrapped around us as we walked home, intoxicated by the smell of the wild herb.

May 8, 1990

The palazzo is completely full of people and has been so for weeks. I have gone from a state of isolation to a throng of people moving through my kitchen in pajamas in the mornings. The challenge of the moment seems to be how to remain centered in my own being with three extra people here, piled on top of the five who live here full time. I come out and stretch canvasses in my nightgown, dribbling tea down my chin. I wear sunglasses in my own kitchen. I gravitate towards painting and writing in the late night hours.

I need to stay up late at night to enter into the deep communication with myself that it takes to pull the images and the words out from my core — the parts of me that surface when I am dreaming. I tell even my favorite people they must leave the room when it's time to write. I have to be super-sensitive to the smallest whisper of the desire to paint or write. With so many people in my most intimate circle, the desire is very softly spoken. It's hard to hear the inner voice when everyone has the TV on or a giant pot of black beans has to be started tonight to feed everybody tomorrow.

It seems that my body has played a little trick on me this time — that I am pregnant again. It is not a good time now — is it ever? I just finished writing an article to submit for publication on creativity and pregnancy. As I re-worked it tonight in a state of pure exhaustion I thought how apropos it is that I am wrestling with the same fears and misgivings that I did almost three years ago.

It is different now, but not easier. There is a big roadblock inside of me about being a mother and really having enough left over for my art, even though it has worked out very well with #1.

Now I haven't actually had a pregnancy test, but I asked one of my spirit guides and she said this was my last baby that they were sending to me and to keep him. Now how can you argue with someone with wings and a cosmic message with your name on it? Enough of being a smartass about this. It simply is not so easy to run out and get an abortion as it once was. I have given birth to a Child of Light and getting an abortion is no longer like stepping on a stray cigarette you found burning on the sidewalk.

Since Alexandra was born I have produced as much really fine work as I have at the greatest peaks of productivity in my life. That's the truth of it all. Motherhood has not interfered with my creativity one bit.

On another subject, I got a very good commission to paint a picture for a Kingmanite — just about as miraculous as the long-awaited freezing over of Hell. I had hung two small jewels of paintings down at my friend Michelle Hofmann, the silversmith's shop. A woman who has just moved here from California saw them and tracked me down to paint a major piece for her new home.

I went to see the space and she told me she would really like something in pastel to go over there. I invited her over to my studio to see more of my work and to give her a price. After much meditative thought I came to a price. I then drove out to Oatman, an old mining town nearby. On the winding road the perfect image came to me. I pulled over to view the magenta beavertail on the side of the road. I tore up a roadmap and worked the drawing out there in the car on the scrap of paper.

When she came over, she was drawn to a huge painting of soft rocks. Could I do something like that? Well, that is exactly the type of image I had gotten in the car. I handed her the torn up map and she loved the drawing. I showed her the range of colors that I work in and said I couldn't paint to anyone else's specifications or the painting would die on me. I had to paint with my colors, not pastels, or I couldn't take the commission. In other words, I told her what I would need to do, colors, sizes and all. I named the price and we struck an agreement. Funny how it is when you sell a piece of your work — everything changes. The canvas is stretched and ready. I begin on the new moon, unless I can't wait. Art abhors a vacuum.

Chapter 15

THE BLACK OGRE
High Desert Gallery . . . Black bean soup . . . The vortex of Kingman . . .
Fluorescent Burning Corpses . . . Dancing in the streets

June 9, 1990

After everything was said and done, it turns out that I was pregnant. I did not, however, choose to listen to some of my feminine spirits. After much agonizing and many tears, Bob and I decided to end the pregnancy. We didn't feel that we had enough to give to another little person. The whole experience was devastating, emotionally, physically, and spiritually, but the fantasy of having a child is vastly different from the reality of another child. We are still very depleted from the birth of Alexandra. I was not willing to sacrifice what I had gotten back of my own life to become The Great Earth Mother. I'd like to do a good job with one child rather than be torn apart trying to give more than I have.

I didn't want to write this down, but I have a commitment to honesty here. I also have a commitment to myself and to my marriage. I can't take on a responsibility that will place a timebomb inside of my relationship to myself or to my husband.

On the creative front, I have finished the commissioned painting for the Montgomerys. It is a magnificent piece. It came out without the usual stress that makes commissioned work so detestable and unsatisfying. I think that's because of knowing my own boundaries and stating them. Hope I get a chance to try that theory out again soon, although my preference is to sell work that I have already produced.

Put an ad in the paper to find two more students.

Also, last week I received a copy of an article that I wrote on the subject of creativity in recovery which got published in a magazine in California. What a high that was! They also printed two photos that I sent them. Two lessons: 1) it pays to follow your most off-the-wall ideas sometimes, and 2) artists must learn how to photograph their own work, no matter how long it takes. I didn't take a photography class. I taught myself with the help of friends and some very patient people who worked in camera stores and photo labs.

Anyway, I was elated to see my stuff in print again. Scared, too. It's self-disclosure on a big scale for me. I didn't want my mother to read it, but it was freeing to write it and after all I let her read it, too.

I have been plagued by terrible nightmares for about two months. Today I stretched a canvas and began to work uneasily on an image of the Black Ogre. There is nothing like painting out the archetype of the Evil that lurks inside of my own unconscious. I just don't seem to have the filters that most people have to stop some of this material from reaching its tentacles up through the plumbing. I wouldn't be happy if it suddenly stopped, however. It is a worse thing for me to be cut off from my own shadow. Still, to have it materialize from the underworld into my own bedroom...

The image is silhouetted against a red background, very simple. He carries a knife and a severed head. My head. My knife. My past life. My current life. A fearsome image and a formidable enemy. Of course this is also my greatest ally. I had to paint him in order to absorb his awesome power into my self rather than be killed by his rage. They are bloodthirsty when ignored, the *brujos*.

There's a spectacular electrical storm going on outside. I want to switch off the computer and move away from the lightning striking so close to my window before I get electrocuted. Strange things often happen when one is tampering with the contents of the unconscious. I fear worse if I try to look the other way.

The storms that rage in the desert are to be experienced in one's lifetime if possible. You can't believe that so much water can come down out of the sky. Ancient memories stored in the cells of mankind are stirred by the real power and fury of nature.

June 12, 1990

The woman who commissioned the painting asked me to write a statement about the piece for her collection. I spent an hour looking at "The Path" to try to find the right words about what I was painting. Here goes:

This painting is a visual statement about the mystical process of moving through different stages of life. The soft rocks first made an appearance in my work in 1988, after the birth of my child. The massive, rounded shapes of intense color grounded me for a deepening of my own experience of life. These rocks are very strong in their softness, inviting one to enter the spaces in-between. My curiosity leads me ever deeper, my spirit and my heart follow close behind.

I chose these jewel-like colors to work with because they are powerfully healing. They are restful, dense and serene. They are the colors of the inner landscape. The golden path represents the desire to go forward, to explore, to learn. It is the golden path of the spirit, because we choose to "walk in beauty," as the Native Americans say. The path itself is our teacher and guide, leading us forward to our next level of experience.

It's a great exercise, trying to put my feelings and thoughts about a particular painting into words. It's challenging, and brings about a certain opening. Maybe it is a sliver of light shining between the left and the right brain. There is an integrating shift — two hands clasping each other, fingers entwined. You can carry more with two hands than one.

June 15, 1990

Came back from Sedona a few hours ago exhausted and ready to fall into bed — hah!

It all began at the airport vortex, which sucked me towards it the moment I drove into town. Without protest I drove up the winding road, pulled off to the side and parked under a tree. I walked up to the brink and said my customary greetings. Suddenly the wind came up and tried to get into me. At first I bridled at the blast of psychic energy I felt, but I quickly realized the source of that energy and allowed the wind to come up inside of me, up my skirt, between my legs and to begin whirling in my womb. I was pleased that it wanted to come into me after the recent physical violence to that part of my body. It did not seem like "sacred ground" in there until I felt the wind coming into me, turning me into a pinpoint vortex.

During the course of my stay I received an unbelievable amount of information regarding the very odd nature of the place where I live and have been able to do so much creative work, which is Kingman, Arizona.

Apparently, there is a powerful vortex created in part by the ancient volcano, now extinct, which forms the ring of mountains around Kingman. The other vibratory energies have been caused by a war between the negative and the positive forces which are actively fighting it out in the psyches of the people who live in Kingman. This switching between the balance of the polarities caused violent shifts in the charge of the atmosphere of Kingman, allowing those who have their finger in the socket, so to speak, to pump out a prodigious quantity of work. Those who would like to sleep here can likewise slip themselves into a stupor of non-growth — Sleepy Hollow.

At certain times the energy whirling in Kingman can make your socks fly off at the dinner table. At other times a catatonia comes down upon the place, palpable as far as the vision can carry you. There is peace here, too, at times, an eternal peace found only in the desert — particularly in an un-chic desert.

I can't begin to lay out the ideas that this being who came by the name of La Marquita had to say in this context. She has pictures, she has words. I plan on working with this new influence to be her storyteller on this plane. I'm going to start on a manuscript on the new moon.

Tonight I heard the coyotes calling all around my bed in the desert. They are her animal, and now my companions for awhile.

July 4, 1990

In a few days I'll open a small gallery in beautiful downtown Kingman. It's been a great education making the arrangements, getting the license, the permits, doing the business cards. I always marvel at how much artists either already know how to do, or can learn to do. If I had to pay someone else to do it all it would cost me a fortune and it wouldn't look the way I want it to.

I'm going to look for a skull to hang up inside to frighten the local Christians, and put in a Mexican chair with a serape draped over it. I'll find some cactus to put in. Maybe even some paintings...

It's working just the same as having a show in any other gallery. Suddenly I have an urge to paint and paint to make new things to put up on the walls. The rent is very inexpensive, so I don't have to become hysterical about sales. The computer is moving downtown also, so it will double as a writing space.

I have a strong desire to return to Santa Fe. There is something I would like to do there — quite a few things, in fact. So while I am here in Kingman I am going to try to get as far into this work as I can. One of the reasons I wanted to come to this god-forsaken place was to continue with this writing. My experience has been that I need to complete what I perceive to be my end of the assignment before I get the cosmic assistance necessary to leap over mountains of obstacles.

There is no way for me to actually get to Santa Fe, either physically or financially. And then there is the issue of my stubborn Aries mother... Well, I'm not going to let reality interfere with my dream. If you allow that, you never get anywhere but the job at the dry cleaners cleaning lint out of the pockets.

Anyway, the most important thing is that I am painting up a storm — as my painting teacher, Dorothy Cannon used to say, "Paint. Just keep painting." Well, it's twenty-one years later and I'm still following her directions. It's the surest path to keep me tucked in close to the source of my guidance.

I got a really beautiful pueblo painting several days ago, that just came tumbling out, as some paintings will, with minimal interference on the part of the artist. I was watching a series of very intriguing videos on Carl Jung, called

The Wisdom of the Dream. There were a number of shots of Taos pueblo. I put the video on pause and sketched around the scratchy areas. Major pain in the ass. As usual, the paintings look nothing like the original. But it's "The Secret Place." Very powerful piece for me — the process and the end result.

July 5, 1990

Now I know I want to leave Kingman, and it's hell waiting to get out of here. Time stretches long each day. I feel as if I am very nearly done here.

I made a commitment to myself to get as far as I can in this journal before my departure. I want to finish this book here in Kingman. The important thing is that I'm leaving. Finishing this will help me make a ceremonial act of closure.

It's been an all-consuming project to live through the waves of change in my life, recording them in my journal. All of this needed to be put in print for artists who needed to know that the process works. There is a force that will put us where we are supposed to be, provide the ways, the means, the cardboard boxes, and the strength. It has to do with following the intuition, believing in it. The Great Spirit is a demanding master, and one who takes all things into consideration.

I am going to try to make a concerted effort to bring myself back into the moment, however, to focus on my gallery. I have practiced quite a bit of selling here in Kingman for myself and for my friend, Michelle, the silversmith. This is an ideal place to practice and to learn. There's no one watching, not much competition, and a little money goes a long way here as far as rent is concerned, at least in the downtown area. I still think this place makes for an ideal artists colony, if the artists could stand the shit-kicker attitude. Fortunately, there are some redeeming kindred spirits here who haven't been totally destroyed by the Union Carbide Scam Wars...

I want to work on a second pueblo painting, but I am having a hard time cranking up my energy. I have the blank canvas out and hanging on the wall looking at me when I am in bed, which is as often as possible. Part of the blockage is this painting of a skull in the prickly pear which is driving me crazy. The skull is beautiful, but I haven't been able to get the background so that I like it. That skull just sits there laughing at me as I change the ground color to adobe to ochre to day-glo pink. The plants have been genetically altered from agave to beavertail to prickly pear. Arrrgh. I hate the damned thing! Some paintings get better the longer you work on them. Some lose more and more of their life. I wonder if this painting is one of the ones that get worse as I go along.

It's certainly a struggling, learning, difficult kind of painting which so often happens after one just comes squirting out. I'll keep at it until I like it. Every few paintings are just like that. Stubborn. Breach births. Ass first.

July 6, 1990

I was driving back from Las Vegas this afternoon, trying not to run into the back of trucks as I composed a statement to include as an official, unsolicited word-bath to accompany my entry into the yearly contest to be chosen as the photo on the cover of the Mohave County phone book. There's usually an exhibit at the Mohave Museum after the competition, the absence of which last year I loudly protested to the local paper. The letter was not published, but a phone company official appeared at my door to explain the omission of an otherwise expected annual event.

I spent many moments trying to charm/cajole/guilt/manipulate the fellow into seeing the importance of their contest and following exhibit for the local artists. Someone has to speak up.

I had a cup of coffee in order to render me able to make a drive in the middle of the night (6:00 a.m.), which has now left me totally wired as if I had several diet pills. I am wasted from no sleep and yet 17 hours later I am still running off in the head. I can't stop thinking about the dreaded vinegaroons that live out here in the desert. Once you've seen one and entertained the thought of one crawling up your leg, you can never really return to the life you formerly lived. I think they are everywhere, and so of course, they are — they fall out of my apron, I find them in my shoes. Some people should never drink coffee.

Bob has been rather blocked in his writing ever since we moved to this place. Kingman depresses him so. This is the kind of place where whatever you are feeling is grossly magnified within a very short time. I know this feeling and the effect too well. We will be having an A.R.T.S. meeting between the two of us tomorrow in order to give us some kind of framework within which we can work. I want another blast of energy.

I got such a boot in the behind when I went to the meetings. I wasn't blocked, I liked my work, but it just allowed something to happen on an inner level that boosted my already overwhelming productiveness. I loved it! It was like a vitamin B shot for my creative drive.

We creative people need to discipline ourselves to work on a regular basis, regardless if the product is good or bad or even complete shit. The blockage just stays there, laughing at us until we look at the empty paper long enough and go through the labor and the pain and drag the stuff out with our own bloody hands.

It's like being pregnant for too long. At a certain point you've got to induce labor. And it shouldn't be much longer than two weeks after it was due. It gets too big. It eats everything that was originally put there by nature to sustain healthy growth. So it is, the sooner the better. It just gets harder the longer we wait.

July 25, 1990

I got really angry in the middle of the night last night. I was picking up the subtle and not-so-subtle "You're not quite a good enough mother" — the so-called joking, cutting stuff that flies through our house. I also woke up this morning with a strong need to come in and write. Thing is, I'm pissed. If I want to keep it all flowing and alive I'll also have to go and tell my clan members that I don't like it. Very scary stuff, standing up for yourself all the time. I can't afford not to. I pay in every area in my life if I try to shirk my duty to myself.

Went to see Sharon the therapist on Monday, after a dream that I was sitting on my therapist's lap sobbing, watching great movements of military troops. When I told her my dream she asked, "Is that where you want to start?" Yes. Let's start with the dream. Again. Not really again because I am always in a new starting place. More has happened, more dreams, more paintings. More of me has surfaced.

We spent some time talking about how to get some more of my intuitive knowledge to link up with my head. I talked about the process of painting my internal life. Talked about using the images to bring some of the forward motion out in front to use as a little light.

The kachina dancers have come to me again and again, in groups and singly to give me helpful information and instructions about how to do certain things — different approaches. I am going to try to record some of these conversations in order to bring them farther out into this world where I can use the information more consciously.

I also want to begin looking for some images to represent saying goodbye to my father and my sister, both very dead. I feel I need to do this in order to go on. It is strange concept for me to need to say goodbye to them because they have lived intact inside of me since they died. I can function pretty well, even dragging them along with me. But there might be a huge storehouse of energy that would open up for me if I dump them. I also sense there would be room for a great expansion of my being if I vacated their pyramids. I also do not want my mother to move in when she dies...

August 7, 1990

Went down and set up the gallery Saturday when Bob was out of town. Looks OK. In fact it looks fantastic. It's just like you stepped off the street in Santa Fe to go in a gallery on Canyon Road, which is where I'd really like to be doing this. The advantage of doing it here is that I don't have to be frightened by actual customers.

I learned something invaluable from the very first person who came in to look at my paintings. She liked them and had thoughtful things to say about them that let me know she had seen a bit of art. After a bit of babbling on she caught herself up short as the sweat ran down from her desert coiffure which was crammed under a greasy cowboy hat that looked as if she had driven over it one too many times (desert chic). She flicked an ash from her hand-rolled cigarette. "I've got just one criticism." Trying to be the Vanna White ultra-Hollywood hostess of Kingman I said as if I was actually interested, "Oh — what's that?" That's where I learned something — DON'T ASK. She didn't like the way one painting was hung over the electrical conduit, crooked. She didn't like the framing, or lack of it. Well, that isn't really a problem. It was her mule-like insistence that I agree with her. Arrrgh. I finally had to tell her clearly that not only were my paintings designed to be hung without frames, I also didn't like frames, I didn't want them, in fact I hated the goddamned things. Then I left in case she couldn't figure out that the conversation was terminated. I have the perfect nature for dealing with the public.

Well, the next night I had a dream in which Geena Davis, the actress, was running the art gallery. When I acted out the various parts of the dream, she had some very interesting things to say. She told me I must be myself in the gallery. It would be very bad for me to try to behave like an ordinary gallery owner. I must be exactly who I am and say exactly what comes to mind rather than being "good" or a good hostess in order to sell my paintings. If I'm done talking to certain people I'm just going to have to tell them that they're welcome to look around but I need to get back to my work. I'm going to keep my painting things down there as well as having the computer, so I can appear to become lost in my work until they leave and I can smudge the evil spirits out of the place. It will simply be a miraculous experience if I actually sell a painting out of the gallery, however, I expect I will get some choice oppportunities to find my boundaries and enforce them i.e.: "Can you please get out of here with that cigarette, you inconsiderate asshole?" I'm glad I'm practicing here.

We're going camping tomorrow with the kid. The plan is to go to Sedona in order to speed up the cosmic spin re: the changes coming in my life. Sedona's good for that.

WARRIOR WOMAN

August 14, 1990

Get me out of here! Get me out of here! Get me out of here! I seem to be suffering from acute Kingmanitis.

It's hard to get used to a major change in the way I work. I had to drag my ass down here to the gallery to use the computer. Dinner's due in an hour and after great deliberation I determined that the best course of action would be to blast out of the house and break my resistance. It takes very, very little resistance to shut down the desire to create. So I said — get up, get out, go do it, now before you just have less and less desire to write. My intention is to buy another computer as soon as I can so that I can continue to step down the hall on nights that I can't sleep in order to work on the journal or more articles. Sober Times, a publication for people in recovery, is going to print one of my articles this month. It's about returning to your creativity after having switched it off. I sent a note saying that I really liked writing the articles and putting in some suggestions for more. She called today to ask for one on keeping a journal as a tool for self-healing. I'm real happy about it. I think that if she called up and asked for a piece on gang banging in the prison system I would say yes. I like seeing my stuff in print. I like it a lot.

So the gallery is all set up. I already don't think I like sharing it with Bob. I don't think he likes sharing his work space either. I mean I'm a very selfish creator/creature and I don't like sharing anything with anyone. Also, because the computer is in here I have to keep the curtains rolled down when we're not here, which rather defeats the purpose and approach to the gallery. I think people should be able to look into the windows to entice them in sooner or later. Also, the door can't be left open for our neighbors to keep an eye on the place when we aren't here for the same reason.

Then there's the matter of working out a new routine — having my paints separated, some at the studio, some here. I think I'm going to start a big painting at the studio to work on, as well as having a smaller one going here at the shop. I have to transport my palette back and forth, and I am on the hunt for an English gardening basket — a "trug," to transport it with less risk of the big splat. I brought my French folding easel that I thought was so unnecessary when Philippe first brought it home. It's travelled everywhere with me the last few years. Now it's here in the gallery. It works great and looks authentically arty.

I'm still floating away on the Castaneda books. I'm on *The Eagle's Gift* now, in slow motion because I really enjoy his journey. I particularly liked the last one, *The Second Ring of Power*. He had wonderful descriptions of women and the entrance into the other worlds. I'm also reading something called *The Little Book of Dreams*, author not remembered right now. I'm stirring everything up in my unconscious, as usual.

Well, I'm on my way home to dish up black bean soup. Recipe follows:

Artist's Black Bean Soup

1 bag black beans, washed and surveyed for imposters
1 onion, chopped up
Good olive oil for sauteeing
1 red bell pepper, chopped up
Spike or salt to taste
Bay leaves, 2 or three
Sliced up Smokie Links if you're non-veg or a smoked
    ham hock if you're a real glutton or turkey franks if you
    are needing something else with your beans

Saute onions in plenty of olive oil. Brown sausages in same mix part way through if you're adding them. Dump in red bells. Chuck in black beans. Put in about four times as much water as beans to start. Turn the heat down to simmer. Check frequently, stir and add gobs of water whenever needed, which will be often. The beans can take up to twelve hours to cook, especially in Santa Fe. Pressure cookers take about an hour and a half. I've tried adding kombu, a Japanese sea vegetable. It's supposed to soften them up faster. Sometimes it works, sometimes it doesn't. The supposedly unhealthy way to cook them is to put in two teaspoons of baking soda. Both supposedly help reduce gas. It can go either way. Maybe not such a good idea to eat these on a first date. Or maybe it's a very good idea. With baking soda you can actually eat your beans without a jackhammer in about two hours. Don't plan a dinner party around these little jokers unless you cook 'em the night before.

If you want them for glorious whole beans rather than soup, with chicken or something meaty, cool them in cold water, then drain. Keeps the skins from cracking. They're so cute! If you want them for soup, adjust liquid by addition or subtraction. Add Spike or salt or low-sodium tamari (Bohemian for soy sauce). If you have used a ham hock you probably won't need salt. Some people put their beans in the blender to make them creamy. Plain yogurt or sour cream can be smooshed in. I don't add it myself.

WARRIOR WOMAN

Good tortillas are de rigueur with this concoction. Spinach salad with grated jicama root, a sweetish poppy seed dressing would make an imaginative partnering. Some favor brown rice as an accompaniment, as you get all the protein you need in a meal by combining this with the cute little black beans. Brown rice can be used and stored in the fridge to be re-heated night after night — the perfect thing for the busy artist who doesn't want to cook every damned night.

August 16, 1990

The foot traffic is slower than slow here at the gallery, so I am able to paint with my left hand and write with my right. I'm working on press releases to the local paper about my marvelous and thrilling new venture, a gallery to make my art accessible to the people of Kingman. They are simply banging on the door to see it.

Anyway, it's great painting here and almost no interruptions. People seem to be a little timid about coming into the cave of an actual stark, raving artist. I don't blame them...the current work in progress is an image of fluorescent burning corpses.

August 24, 1990

The kid's asleep, Joanna's zonked out on the couch, Bob's out of town. I haven't been able to work more than a few minutes since the husband and the babysitter left, so we brought Mac home from the office and threw my dripping paintings in the back of the van. Sometimes nothing works better than working at home, i.e., when there's no outside help with the little beast.

The piece I've been working on is the "Burning Corpse." This was up on my easel in the gallery last week. I wish I had had a hidden video camera to record the various reactions of people peeking in the door to see what was on fire. It was a great study of human expression. There were masks of horror, coolness, loss of words. It's a good way to a) strike up a conversation or b) stop one before it starts.

Anyway, the conflagration is now in my bedroom where I can study it at length. This one burning body is the symbol of my dead sister and my father. I am exorcising them from their condo in my psyche. The body is luminous turquoise surrounded by cleansing flames. The atmosphere is purple black. There is a large upside-down funnel of smoke which sucks their spirits up and out of their bodies and my soul.

I am going to take it/them to my therapist and do some active imagination incantations with her acting as the witness. After all, it was she who notified me of their stinking presence in my being. She told me I could not get There lugging their bodies, being shamed by their voices. Going through the experience of the death of family members, one thinks of the Navajo horror of the dead. They have an abject fear of the dead entering into them at the moment of death. I have come to see their point. Hence, a ritual burning is in order for the health of my soul.

My appointment for this event is the day before I go to Santa Fe to see the burning of Zozobra — something I think every city should celebrate. Zozobra started out as Old Man Gloom, but for many he is much more than that. He represents everything we should cast off in our lives. Bacchanalian fiestas of this ilk really flip the bird at the white bread, castrated automatons that many of us have become after the spiritual, physical, and psychic upheavals af the sixties. Thank God I grew up then instead of now! Life pales for me when I get too cut off from my pagan roots.

I have been wanting and needing to attend Zozobra since the death of my father. I need to commemorate the passing of the Old Ones — I never got to dance his death out of me.

August 25, 1990

Since all my support system (husband, childcare-giver) is gone I also haven't been able to go sit the gallery. I mentioned my absence from the gallery to Bob in a guilty fashion and he said how easy it is to take the fun out of it by thinking that way. True! And of course the minute we start to do any kind of business we shouldn't be having fun anymore, or be relaxed, be ourselves. It wouldn't be "professional." If I'm not professional, I won't be as valuable or believable. People would know that I'm a fraud — that I have no right to be doing this.

When I was doing interior design in Los Angeles I had to deal with feelings of this sort all the time. Any minute I was afraid I would be unmasked. My right to make mistakes, to not know, to not care was revoked. I had big headaches most of the time I was working, because I was trying so hard to look like a designer. I know that I am not the only person who ever felt this way. No wonder it's so hard for us to step off the conveyor belt to try something new.

Went to a great street dance in downtown Kingman last night. The night was a warm blanket. Wild Oats, one of the local groups, was playing wonderful tunes cranked up just right for dancing. There were the usual older couples who dance like they've been practicing for the last forty-five years. Smiling, they float by, enjoying every dance. In general though, it seems to be hard for people to get up and dance, especially when no liquor is being served. The street was full of little kids, however, and me dancing with Sasha and Joanna. Some places you go to and the minute the music starts you can hardly find room to dance. A.A./ A.C.A. dances are like that. Well, we had a beautiful time anyway. I wish they did it every weekend in the summer. Kingman might even become an attraction...nahhh.

September 3, 1990

I'm trying to work with a two-and-a-half year old hanging from my neck. It's not as hard as you would think, and it's even kind of cozy. There's a spectacular thunder storm going on outside — lightning, banging, tomato-colored mud flash-flooding by. I'm eavesdropping on a phone conversation about the break-up of a couple I like very much. Not many stay together.

I've spent a lot of time fantasizing about travelling around the world, or what's left of it, leaving someone to sell my paintings at my intimate and hugely successful gallery in Santa Fe. For some this fantasizing would seem to be a waste of time; for me it is a road map. By exiling myself to Kingman, I have proven that I can paint anywhere. Have supplies trucked in by llamas, burros, elephants. But Capri would be nicer — or the rancho in New Mexico.

I'm spending a long time incubating my next article, the one on journal writing and recovery.

It reminds me of a story from when I was eleven-years old. My parents and I were going to Munich for a few months. When we were leaving I went to lock my studio door. My parents said no, no, no. So I took my diary into which I had poured all my most secret thoughts, fears, hopes and despair, and stashed it into a locked file box. Then I put it into my closet and locked it.

When we returned from Germany, to my horror, the closet door was open wide, the door removed from its hinges. The file box had been smashed open and the diary opened and read. There were things in there I didn't want a living soul to know about, and my sister, knowing this, had pillaged my most private things. I realized then that she was my sworn enemy — a real danger to me. She and her deceptively sweet husband blackmailed me for years afterwards, threatening to reveal the contents (the romantic/sexual fantasies of an eleven-year-old) to my mother. They used blackmail to get me to take money out of my mother's purse.

Think about this when you begin to write. There are people out there who will go to any length to find out what you are writing in that little book. You don't even think they've noticed. Most of them put it back carefully just the way they found it so they can look again and again, and you will never know that they are prying into your private life in this way. I must say, I have not one bit of respect for anyone who engages in this practice. No one with the true soul of an artist can do that — just the wanna-be's and never-will-be's. Avoid them like the plague. It's something they never seem to be cured of. Twelve years later my sister was still climbing into my window to go through the papers on my desk. I finally moved out of my parents home to protect myself from her.

With this in mind, it is astonishing that I continued to use my journal as a sanity-searching tool in spite of her invasiveness. I wrote more defiantly. I hid it better. I don't think that we should stop doing something that is so grounding, so healing for us. It's just wise to make a safe place for yourself. Anyway, I write honestly on a regular basis. I leave no feeling unexplored — no words unsaid. I still recommend keeping a journal to those trying to find themselves and their path in a cruel and beautiful world.

Enjoying Natalie Goldberg's *Writing Down the Bones*. It's a well-made tool for writers — painters, too.

September 10, 1990

We returned to Santa Fe for Fiesta and the burning of Zozobra. A gigantic figure resembling a menacing man is burnt every year in the city at the foot of the Sangre de Cristos. It is something I wanted to do as part of my goodbye to my dead father. As the time for the burning drew near a group of us climbed on top of the roof of our friends Art and Kay Lofton's adobe. A frenzied storm was threatening to cut loose — lightening was crashing, thunder rolling. Like people from a primitive tribe, we awaited the cathartic flames, burning away all that we wish to see burned.

After what seemed like hours, total darkness engulfed us. At last we saw the fire spirit begin his dance. On and on he danced as we ached for the flames to start. All of Santa Fe was screaming — "Burn him! Burn him!" We were hoarse with our efforts. As Zozobra was lit on fire, the crowd let out the ancient howls that rise up from the solar plexus. It was a frenzy of destruction. As Zozobra moaned, waving his arms and fighting the battle he loses every year, the rain began to fall in torrents. The fire and the rains. It was a good celebration, worthy of a fallen giant. Goodbye, Dad.

Chapter 16

COYOTE APPEARS
The dead . . .

October 12, 1990

Tonight a hole in the shape of a coyote ran across the street as I came home in the vibrant darkness of the desert. Last week as I drove through the wasteland I saw an eagle standing on something dead and bloody on the side of the road. If I had known he wanted a ride I would have stopped to pick him up. I have friends everywhere.

These damned Dead People! For perhaps two months I have struggled with these corpses in my studio. They have changed colors, identities, feelings, heads. I have entered a creative dead space since getting involved with them. Some part of me is dying with them. I can hardly paint them, and yet like most dead people, you can't just leave them laying there in your room — they require some disposal, a ceremony, some acknowledgment. I don't know what they want from me — they never say! On my part, I want them to be dead and to let go of me... these stinking corpses.

I have no desire to paint or write. Reading's good. Channelling has produced some very inspiring information. La Marquita told me to goof off. A lot. I look off into the distance at the strange way the light moves across the expanses. It's hypnotic — long distance gazing. I prefer it to making art.

I seldom go to the gallery. It is physically painful to me to be exposed to the public at random for several hours in a row. I can't be charming for too many consecutive hours. It makes me sick. I know having my own gallery is the right idea. I'd like to have someone else to sit it.

October 18, 1990

An extraordinary thing happened to me today. The phone rang and there was a man I didn't know on the other end asking me to write for his magazine in Los Angeles. He had seen several of my pieces in Sober Times and loved them. His publication doesn't have cash to pay for articles. I have a firm policy of getting compensated for my work, so perhaps I'll work out a trade for an ad for this book.

When I got off the phone with him I was flooded with ideas about writing projects, painting energy (The Warrior Woman painting is next, I think...), plans

118

for dinner parties, hope and a general sense of well-being. So here I am tonight, totally wired up because someone in another state read my piece and thought it was good. I had no shyness or reserve about asking him if they paid or if they would be willing to publish shots of my art work. This contributes to my grand scheme of creating a name for myself as an artist, getting my paintings seen by as many people as possible, and creating a market for all the many pearls that drop from my lips about art. It feels great. People will see my work! This is a special way for me to have an exhibit and also have a chance to plant a few choice ideas out in the world.

When I was finished talking with this editor, we struck up the subject of how to go about publishing this. I'd like to get it out by next spring. I've worked on this manuscript for five years. I have 39 years of information and inspiration to pass on. I want to get this one out and jump on the next jaguar that comes out of the bushes.

My current painting plan is to stretch another 4' x 6' canvas to use for the Warrior Woman kachina. I feel I'm going to be needing her medicine soon, although I don't yet have a clue yet as to why. I'm going to get a canvas ready so when she wants to come out, she doesn't have to wait for me to stretch her canvas. Then I'm going to have a whole mess of people over to our house to look at my paintings and tell stories and eat black beans. Come on over to my house, we'll have New Mexican food — blue corn tortillas, black beans, green chile — *muchos colores.*

This is my art world. I'm 39 now, so I have a right to come through with a battering ram. Today it's okay — someone out there likes my stuff. Hell, someone out there has even seen my stuff. Sometimes I wonder if I'm not safer here. No doubt. The place is full of throwbacks, pencil-necked geeks, door-knob heads, rednecks, mountain men, bikers with no front teeth, as well as some very wonderful folks (not quite as easy to find.) But there's no pressure. No pressure at all.

Anyway, people have sought me out here. I've gotten several calls and some lovely letters from around the country just to do with those three articles. The best thing I probably ever did for my painting was learn to write — and take photographs of my work. And get paid.

I also don't grovel anymore or show up with my portfolio and paintings at the galleries of various people who will very soon be ignoring me or handing me a shit sandwich or asking me to re-do that tree in desert colors. I mean, what are those — desert colors??? Road-kill red? The color of undigested berries or house cats who stayed out too late in coyote scat? The burned-out yellow of dead abandoned dogs who have gone too long without water in the badlands? That color makes a nice generic desert weed color a TV painter can use on his fan brush to demonstrate how to paint bushes. What the hell are desert colors? I have to induce a near hallucinogenic state to see the colors I use to paint the desert. It's not easy without the aid of my old chemistry set.

I went out last night into the desert and there was no moon. The Big Dipper — and I mean I do mean big — was resting its bottom two stars on the top of the mesa in back of the house. There are things you can see here that you just can't see anywhere else. I've lived in Paris, in Munich, London, Mexico City, and travelled to many more places than that. You'll never see the stars so brilliant in any of those man-made wonders. The desert sky is just one of those naturally magical things. There is a Power greater than me. Lets me see things like that all the time. There's not much to get in the way of one's line of vision here.

October 19, 1990

Today Sharon, the woman I trade painting lessons for therapy with, came over to paint. I had stretched a big canvas yesterday for the Warrior Woman, and called her up — I'm ready to start a Big One. Le-e-e-e-t's paint!

This painting has been incubating for a very long time. The great thing about keeping this kind of written account of the ins and outs of my art life is that I can go back through and get an overview of the entire birthing process. I usually even know when conception took place. Can you say that about yourself?

Anyway, I've only put in about two and a half hours and she's very near completion. Some paintings come out like that. I haven't gotten in the way. I just stand on a chair and try to be a clear channel — i.e.: get clear out of the way. I want to paint morning, noon and night, so I do. You always think — if I don't hold something back, if I hurry up and paint this way, so fast, so strong, what will I do next? Crap, isn't it? Doesn't much take into account the last 21 years of steady painting. Well, maybe I'll run out of gas in another 20 years. Maybe I never will.

Anyway, the ever-helpful human brain is always at the ready with useless and strangulating insults. It's not your mother putting you down anymore, you know... this stuff just pours out of our own little factories of negativity, uninvited whenever the door opens a crack. That's why I like to listen to music when I paint — keeps the natives busy.

This week I'm going to talk to some friends about self-publishing or whatever else comes up on the get-it-out-there circuitry. I'm going to make up a generic ad, camera ready, that can be placed in the papers I might write for that advertises my forthcoming book (due in the summer?).

I'll offer to send them material in exchange for running my ad. I'll leave an address for advance ordering, and see what happens. I can't believe how brave I am. *Cojones!*

There is a big opening party for the little complex of shops where I have my gallery next weekend. It's good to already have the gallery set up and ready to go. It's like I'm used to doing shows except I don't have to cart everything to the exhibit or take it down when it's over and I'm already bone-tired.

I know the paintings look beautiful. Now I just drive around town passing out invitations to people I like. There's no bullshit to put up with about what I can show or not show, what they're going to choose or reject, what I'm going to charge and how much of that I have to give to someone else. I don't have to act right — whatever that is — or be a good girl. Nothing! It's all mine, hung right where I think it should be hung. I don't have to schlepp anything down there, even. I'm going to go down there tomorrow and sit the gallery in the afternoon. I'll take my articles about starting A.R.T.S. in Santa Fe, and start the general article about A.R.T.S.. I'll have some more things in my repertoire to submit for publication.

I started to read an absolutely fascinating book, *People of the Blue Waters*, by Flora Grigg Iliff. She was school teacher to the Hualapai and Havasupai Indians around the turn of the century. A likely explanation as to the incredible negative vibrations one feels here in Kingman was mentioned in the "Mohave Daily Miner" in the 1890s. When the Hualapai and Havasupai tribes were crushed by the United States Government, they were herded into Kingman in disgrace. They then proceeded to use their shamans to engage in every means available in the unseen world to curse the area, perhaps the inhabitants as well. This directly parallels my feelings that this once idyllic area was transformed into a swirling negative power vortex by the acts of man. In the "Miner" which was published at the time reporters hinted at black magic being practiced heavily in the area. The Ghost Dance apparently was danced here at length and in earnest, in the hopes that the Anglos would disappear from the face of the earth. Relatives who had gone on to another world would return, young, healthy and happy. The local Kingmanites circulated petitions at that time to try to put a stop to the practice of Indian magic. Nothing has changed! Finding this piece of information has confirmed my psychic impressions of Kingman. The Earth Mother has brought many people here to try to counterbalance these terribly negative imprints left here from that time, like toxins leaking into the underground water. Still, I don't know how long I can stand it here. Non-nourishing, non-stimulating. Sometimes I do the Ghost Dance here, too.

WARRIOR WOMAN

I bought a sparkling crystal that was pulled from a mine in the Hualapai Mountains here in Kingman. The Hualapais are a pretty good source of crystals. The stones have a distinctive orangey-apricot color. Powerful stone medicine here. The Kingman turquoise is stunning, too. Unique. Good to put next to the bed at night. My Warrior Woman kachina is there also, right now, keeping watch while I sleep, protecting me in the Dreamworld. Anyway, some artists need to sleep with their subjects.

October 28, 1990

We're getting into my own season of el Dia de los Muertos. Today is the birthday of my dead sister, Sharon. Tomorrow is the tenth anniversary of her long, drawn-out death of cancer. Halloween is coming. My mother dreamt that my father was in bed with her, caressing her hand. This is the time of the year when the veil between the worlds is most easily penetrated, so it doesn't surprise me that he visits her now. Perhaps I will think of something to do for the occasion — like invite the dead to leave. I used to like having them around, but they talk too damn much.

The opening at the gallery went beautifully. I was certifiably insane before it started. Lost my keys and had to break in by climbing through the window. I felt the need to insult a visitor to the gallery. Was simply charming to crowds of people. Nothing out of the ordinary. Sold nothing! Am I surprised? No. But I don't like it.

I think it will be much more gratifying to open a gallery in a place where there is some kind of more widely spread appreciation for art. Still, it was divine to have many, many people come to see my paintings. It was also very gratifying to be part of one of the most innovative cultural events in Kingman. Frustrating, too. I went to the shop the next day in case there were more people coming by to see the place. Four of my friends came by. We had all expected a big crowd. Often no-one comes for many hours on end and I leave in boredom and disgust. I can get all of my writing done there, however.

While I was there waiting for my admiring public, I managed to compose a "deal letter" (small-potatoes version...) to send to the editor of Athena, a magazine for women who are recovering from abusive relationships. The letter is regarding the trade of articles for ad space. I stated that a trade was in keeping with my policy of always being paid for my work, as well as what he is trying to teach his readership — a sense of self-value. I'll type it up tomorrow and send it off before I do any writing on the actual article. The plan this week is to do that, locate the simplest source for developing black and white contact sheets to get a good shot for this paper, and work on my pre-publication ad for my book. It's a real challenge doing this type of prep work when you live in the sticks. Also a real chore when you're a right brain type.

The extraordinary thing about the last week is that everyone in the house was more or less deathly ill, leaving me without even a babysitter. Still, I managed to finish the exquisite painting of the Warrior Woman (If nobody else shows up to praise your work, it's very important to do it for yourself!), hand write all the invitations, get the show ready, pin up my hair, break in the window and smile. I also had a very good time doing it. I did have to yell at Bob that it was the day of my show and I was not going to take care of anything for anyone else, i.e.: wake up all night long with the kid who was sick during the night and also get up early in the morning to take care of her. I would do one or the other, not everything. Sometimes I just have to lie down on the floor and have a proper tantrum to straighten out my priorities — as well as the priorities in my family.

November 2, 1990

In honor of the Day of the Dead, I have begun the next painting in my series of dead people. I started a piece with myself with a halo of jimson weed flowers surrounded by three skeletons at a fiesta. They look as if they are having a wonderful time. I have always admired the Mexican recognition and celebration of death. Here we are hardly allowed to cry after even the most devastating losses. We seem to have lost the art of grieving. As a nation we are phobic about death. It is not admitted into our culture as part of the continuum of life, and those who grieve too loudly, too publicly are shunned and feared. We do not know how to die any more than we know how to live! The grieving are tranquilized, calmed. Always the edge is dulled. So it is in the everyday life of the average American. Turn on the TV and live through the characters. Whatever you do, remove yourself from the firsthand, bleeding, crying, laughing, dancing, screaming experience of life or death.

I am working on this series of paintings to help myself reach the next level of acceptance about death and dying. I'm certainly not doing it for commercial acceptance. I started the piece while Sharon, the woman I trade with for therapy, was here for her painting lesson. It was she who got me on to the idea that I needed to let go of my sister and my father in order to go on with my life — at least at the level that I want to live it on. I'll go see her next week to do some verbal work, maybe role-playing, now that she's seen the images. Then I'm going to sew up their mouths and burn them, like proper dead people.
November 6, 1990

WARRIOR WOMAN

Last weekend we went to Seattle for a "recovery conference" It was wonderful just to be around people, listen to them talk. Bob spoke about how much he loved me, and I felt very, very important to him and wanted. He also announced to this rather large crowd that I was writing a book and that we were publishing it next year. The adrenaline rush was quite intoxicating.

When we flew out of Bullhead City on our way home, I looked out and saw Laughlin, Nevada, all pastel neon softly shimmering on the Colorado River. I remarked how much more beautiful it looked than it really is. We returned home to the desert to see the Big Dipper winking on top of the mesa, welcoming us home. I wondered what the jack rabbits were still doing out in the desert, which is growing colder everyday. Sometimes I can feel how much I love it here, and I know I will miss it when I go.

November 7, 1990

When I pulled out of the driveway this morning, tumbleweeds were bouncing along wildly across the path of my car. A gift from Bob, a big earthy-colored Indian blanket coat came for me in the mail two days ago — just in time. The weather has swung into the high desert winter. The cold comes snapping through the air and billowing up from the earth. It's the time to lock yourself up and work on introspective projects. Time to get out the long underwear that is my trademark through the winter. I sleep in it, wear it out to the market and to restaurants. One can fully enjoy the winter with an overly long thermal underwear top, all-cotton from Penney's and a grand pair of Sorrel's. It doesn't translate well into big-city life, but it's heaven out here.

I'm crawling along with the Day of the Dead painting. The curious quality of deadness that comes over me as I paint along in this series is oddly fascinating and flatly uninteresting to me all at the same time. I wonder what kind of growth will come from this cycle of paintings. I no longer want to go along with my mother when she dies. Another change is a tremendous surge of the life force, like water breaking through a dam. There is much I want to do. I want to get on the back of the spirit horse and ride like a wild thing. I want to have no more to do with the dead.

Next week we are going to go to Lost Wages to look at computers. We are working towards getting my own so I can work when Bob is working, although I am primarily a writer of the vampiric ilk. I mostly get the itch at night. But for the more businesslike part of the writing, ads, articles, etc., the day seems to suit me just as well. I have more or less a direction, a list, a time frame in which I plan to move over the next six-ish months.

It's a whole shitload of work, but I work very smoothly and steadily under pressure. The more I have to do, the more I do. The photography for the ads and the ads themselves are the next projects I have laid out. Then there is a series of articles I want to write and verbal agreements to work out for trade. Then I am going to sit back and watch what happens as the ads begin to come out.

Somewhere in all this from time to time come the real or imagined fears of being judged and criticized. I imagine the horror that will come from my mother or various friends at the time that this work is actually in print. Most artists and writers have to struggle with this same army of demons, made up of a thousand projections from the conscious and unconscious. What will my pastor think? He'll probably stop having sex with you. What will my mother think? She'll find out who I really am and realize she always disapproved of me, despised me. No wonder all my relationships ground down into the dirt. Well, I answer myself, I'm going to do it anyway.

I'm not going to clean it up or censor it. It's me, and it's about me. I have worked very long, very hard, to achieve real expression of myself. The publication of this will mark the end of my behaving differently in different places. I don't do that very much, but I've made a decision to pull out the rest of the stops and attend all the dances as Me. I'm done with even the little holding back. I love who I have become over the last fifteen years, and even more who I have had the courage to become over the last ten. Courage is not the absence of fear, because I am full of it. For me it is doing things even though I am very afraid.

My gift to myself for all this dedication and work is more personal freedom, more risk, more adventure. My sister has been dead for ten years now. She died the day after she turned 37. I am 39 this year, and I have barely scratched the surface. Don't get me wrong — I have done it ALL. And I mean ALL. What I'm talking about is going on to the next level of vitality and life. I'm on my way. When this manuscript finishes itself, it will mark the end of many assignments — the end of an era. I am going to step out of my skin and get moving onto some different planes of experience and understanding. I'm leaving this reality and segueing into other worlds. The desert is good for this type of discorporation, dematerialization. There is little here to define me, little to drain me or hold me in place. What little there is is like the tumbleweed blowing into my path for a moment and careening off into the cosmos with the wind spirits. It's here one beat of the drum and gone. Totally gone.

Chapter 17

SOLD
Dorothy . . . Tribal life . . .

November 10, 1990

We sold the house yesterday. I was so cranked up last night I couldn't sleep. We also bought me my own computer to better help me crank out the rest of this manuscript. Moving is a time for finishing, and that's what I'm gearing up for here.

The new Mac is in the middle of my drawing table with newly designed headers for my upcoming column for the news-mag, Athena. The various mock-ups for my ad are also floating around in front of my face. There are a number of the big blank drawing pads that I use, two medium-sized yellow legal pads that I do my writing notes on, my customary 5"x8" blank black book, of the type I have been filling up steadily over the last fifteen years. My incredibly gooped-up palette that I never clean that looks like a topographical map of the badlands is glistening seductively, balanced on Mac's little umbilical cords. There is a beautiful postcard-print of a woman from the tomb of Tutankhamen, a photo of an entry into my black journal (Dead People), and a copy of a book titled *Shapeshifters, Shaman Women in Contemporary Society* (a phone book, perhaps?). There's a sculpturally exquisite black Italian lamp of the type that I can never resist and a half-chewed up piece of dried papaya — the kind of treat I often give to Sasha.

This is very typical of the array of stuff I generate around myself. I keep favorite working materials always within easy reach. I never put it all away because of the energy it takes to find it all and get it out again. Some people thrive artistically on neatness — I do not. Everything is pretty spare and empty so that I don't have to spend very much time cleaning — I'm terrible at that and resent doing it — but the stuff that turns me on creatively is scattered about in such a way that my eyes always rest on something I find beautiful or intriguing. Art supplies are kept out on the work surfaces so with little or no thought I can let things seep out with no special effort.

Not last night but the night before, I dreamed that I was digging in some dirt and began to uncover ancient artifacts. The first were Chinese *netsuke*. There were little carvings of monkeys doing hear no evil, speak no evil, see no evil. There were lots of Egyptian plaques and jewels. Bob was across the counter saying put it back, put it back. I said with conviction as he put on a beautiful necklace with a saber tooth mounted on it, "Look down at that necklace! That's your old necklace from before! These are our old things — they belong to us. That's why I know where to look for them." As he looked down he realized that what I was saying was true. This was his necklace from long, long ago. I then came upon some small gold rings. They only fit up to the first joint on my little finger. They used to fit me, like other rings I had dreamt of before. I decided to give two to two women who were there with me, one of whom was a sternly disapproving history teacher who was threatening me with a test for which I was not prepared. I turned and dropped one of the rings. It began to bounce on the floor, but it didn't stop. It just kept bouncing and bouncing. I recognized that it was a magic ring and did not want to be given to anyone else. Suddenly it turned into a tiny golden butterfly.

My mother came into my studio today. She was gazing at the "Warrior Woman" painting when I left the room. I didn't stop to see if she had noticed the "Day of the Dead" painting in progress on the easel. I wonder what she thinks when she sees such things, but I make a disciplined point of never ever asking. I seldom want to know what anyone thinks of my paintings anymore.

In my parents' home in Cambria, I hung my painting, "The Woman Who Is the River." While I was flitting around the Southwest in my truck my mother had it removed from my room. My mom was still drinking at that time. She thought it was a painting of a dead woman in a river. To me the woman represented the river of life, the mother of the waters. There was another painting of a woman and her dream-horse emerging from the sea. My mother thought the woman looked as if she were starving and also had that painting moved. It was a painting that represented the emergence of a new self for me — a very important piece of work for my soul! People really see exactly what is inside of themselves when they look at other peoples' art work. It's all just one big Rorschach test. If they knew this, they probably would say a good deal less about art within earshot of anyone else.

Fortunately, I have trained the people around me to keep most of their comments to themselves, so these interpretations came to me second and third hand. Still, what if I allowed myself to be influenced by their opinions? Train the people around you to zip it up unless it is a teacher who actually knows something about what she or he is talking about — not all of them do.

November 11, 1990

Last night I worked on my ad for the book. I learned something very important while I did it. Some people find it very hard to write copy — I do not. But as I was looking over my words it came to me that I should write exactly what I would really, really like to hear someone else say about me and my work. It's not so hard when approached in that way. If you sit there and get into thinking that people are going to know that you are such a fat-head, that you wrote this about yourself, it gets more difficult by the moment.

I also stuck in all the things that would make me want to read the book. It's a great exercise. Reveals a lot about where you are with how you feel about yourself, if you can stand to examine such things (i.e., scorpions under smooth, warm rocks...). Obviously, there are days to engage in this sort of thing and days to avoid it, at least if your primary objective is sales rather than suicide.

After I was mulling all this around it dawned on me that this is what I do when I am selling other people's things. I pull out all the stops. I positively gush over their talent and worth. Then I decided that's precisely what I need to do with my own work — gush unashamedly. This is something I have never done. Too polite. Wouldn't want to embarrass anyone or put someone on the spot. Well, as I write it occurs to me that there may be a way to do that and also do it in a way that I can stomach. There's always the vomit factor to take into consideration. I do think that there's a way to solve this. I'm going to work on it and write some dialogue. I just can't lie.

I've talked to Michelle Hofmann about coming with me when I open up another gallery. I'm afraid she's heading off to Colorado on her next adventure, however. Too bad. Her work is stellar and having a gallery with her would solve the dilemma of having a space to show my work on an on-going basis where I am autonomous. This way I wouldn't have to be tied down to being indoors in a gallery. I could be out goofing around, riding horses, and picking up bones in the desert.

November 12, 1990

An avalanche of change is coming. The earth has begun to shift, inside and out. My animal self is full of nameless fears. My body is quivering inside, in the area of my solar plexus. I wonder what will be torn away and what will be left.

There is a change of residence coming, happily so in many ways. Estella, our much-loved childcare giver, is very suddenly gone. I was terribly sad to see her go. But there is more, much more to go, and I know it. I know it in the same way that I knew it before we were ripped out of our home in Santa Fe. It's an avalanche and it's heading our way.

There is a prayer I like for these times of violent change:

128

Great Spirit, thank you for what you have given me,
Thank you for what you have taken away,
And thank you for what you have left me.

The fascinating thing to me has always been, how do I know that a time of radical transition is about to begin? I know it six months or more before the sands begin to shift. I start to "get ready" — an elusive term because I don't consciously know what I am getting ready for.

I find myself frantically getting rid of things, recycling clothes, dumping perfumes, pawning books. I sell twenty, thirty, forty books I no longer pick up to read, and trade them for two or three really beautiful art books, i.e., Diego Rivera.

People go, too. That part hurts. The people who used to be part of my life and my circle of love are unceremoniously yanked, ripped and torn out of my life. Some know how to let go graciously. With love and good wishes, we wave goodbye to each other at the dock. Others have to pick a fight in order to break the tie. They give me the finger and leave spitting at me. Sometimes I wonder if it will come to that with my mother. I wonder about everyone I know. The path gets narrower. Few will come along.

Then there is the strange other side, where I am moved to acquire new things, costumes, props, lights, furniture, computers, radar detectors, answering machine with beeperless remotes and phone-changeable messages, big rubber boots, giant down coats and quilts. By the time the earth starts moving I am sitting on top of the landslide screaming and bucking, with everything I will need for the next indicated life.

The thing here is to not disrupt the creative momentum more than I have to. Sometimes the disruption is more lengthy than I care for although during those times I usually set myself to a task in different media, like starting the A.R.T.S. meeting in Santa Fe, or getting pregnant and hatching a little person. The great canvas of life. Enough joking — I have a lot of anxiety as I am thrown into the hellish and unmerciful fires of change. What parts of me will be burned away in the flames? I know it is going to hurt. Who and what will be left? Anything? Who will I be next?

People who go through this process every few years will know what I am talking about. Not everybody does this in life. Some find their 1 1/2 acres, settle down and homestead. They get buried under the peach tree with their mate and their kids standing around. My pattern of growth and learning is more flamboyant, covered with flames and lit-up on stage so everyone around for several miles can see me crying and cracking, burning and breaking. Here comes another one.

WARRIOR WOMAN

November 14, 1990

This will have to be quick and on the run, as everything has to be since the babysitter flew the coop.

The sky has been full of sundogs the last week. They are small rainbows formed by ice crystals in the desert clouds. I marvel at their perfection and beauty, and take them as signs of the changes that are coming.

I have little time to paint this week as I am just getting used to being on the total mommy track again. Next week, come hell or high water, I paint. My energies are much divided into mental and physical departures. I am spending much time going through boxes and dumping stuff — re-cycling it, really. Disruption lies ahead. I'm going to focus my energy and my creativity on this little Mac and finish the most pressing tasks.

The kid's crying. I'm off for now.

Later That Same Eon..

I went into the nursery to find my husband completely and totally under Sasha's bed. She told me in her two-year-old voice to get oudda here. I know a chance when I see one.

Before I began writing this eve I was drawn over to the Medicine Cards, the wonderful non-tarot cards by Jamie Sams. I have been using the eagle as my animal ever since I saw the one standing by the side of the road in the desert. I drew the turkey tonight which is the card of the giveaway. It's funny because this is what I am doing right now. Clothes are going — who should they go to? Many of them no longer suit me. I am changing too fast. There are others who will like these beautiful things that used to belong to me. I find myself decisively choosing strong pieces of clothing and things to use in my new life, whatever that will be.

Yesterday or so, Peter Alsop and his wife, Ellen Geer, came through for a visit and to see paintings. It's like pioneer life here. When an interesting woman comes through I grab her and study her. We talked about what we are reading, seeing, doing. I recognized her face immediately from some sketching I had done of her when she was acting at the enchanted Theatricum Botanicum in Topanga Canyon in Los Angeles. It must have been about ten years ago. I went there many times to see them do *Midsummer Night's Dream* and whatever else they had to offer. It was good though to have a brainy and bright one come through with a transfusion. It was splendid to have Peter here as himself and as a man for Bob to bump shoulders with.

Their children were so lit up from inside and so intelligent. It was a rare treat in Kingman to see such a whole and lovely family. I referred their Willow to Dorothy Cannon as a teacher in L.A.. What a gift she is for kids — me, too. I miss her and would give anything to be able to go and paint with her a few times a week. Fourteen years in her company was hardly enough. Beware magical teachers. You'll miss them too much.

Right now, with all the movement happening and much more to come, I would love to be able to go and drink tea with her and Mindy, Trudi, Dahna, and her cat. Some people are very stabilizing even in the midst of a hurricane. You can stop in their circle of strength and affection and just be all right breathing. You don't have to do anything else.

There is much of her inside of me, but I would like to go right now to her house that is all a studio, cluttered with the things of making art. Everywhere you turn is something else to try — etching, papier-mache, colored glass, inviting scraps of wood, a model. And always good conversation and beautiful classical music. And herb tea. You could learn to cook just going there and painting, with all the talk of food and the good things of life. I have laughed a lot there — cried, too.

She caught me when I was 18, fresh out of an abortion clinic and raw. I was living in a home full of practicing alcoholics and addicts. There was Dorothy, like a beacon in the dark, telling me to paint, just paint. She also liked my writing and told me to keep doing it. I would cry and she would bring me tea and pieces of bread she had baked. Honey, too. Honey was big at Dorothy's. She always told me to eat breakfast. "You can't paint if you don't eat breakfast." I pass that truism on to all the artists and writers in the galaxy. Eat breakfast. Dorothy said so. Not everybody is lucky enough to have such a teacher in their lives.

November 18, 1990

Everybody's asleep! Time for me to go to work. Since the addition of another computer in our house I can work whenever there's a lull. My phone time has dropped 75 percent. Talking on the phone siphons off the drive to write, to communicate.

Last night we took Sasha to one of those kiddie pizza parlors. As the people were screaming and scrambling all over us I said to my quaking self, "This is no place to come if you have boundary issues." Then I thought, "I don't have boundary issues, I have boundaries." Don't come to places like this if you have boundaries, because these other people do not. They crawl and creep all over you, elbow you, stare at you and guzzle beer by the pitcherful. Believe me, boundaries work better if both teams are playing by the same set of rules.

WARRIOR WOMAN

Since the babysitter has gone I've had a hard time painting, although there are still some parts of my "Day of the Dead" painting that are brewing. I mentioned this to Bob and he pointed out how much writing I've been doing. So I've made a choice and at least the creativity is still pouring out.

Got a letter from the editor of the magazine that publishes my stuff asking me to go ahead and write the article on A.R.T.S. that I wanted to send to them. It's a tremendous opportunity for me and for the A.R.T.S. program, as the readership is made up primarily of people in recovery programs of all sorts. I'll put in a sample format and people can get these meetings started all over the country. I want to write one about A.R.T.S. in general and one about starting A.R.T.S. in Santa Fe.

The baby woke up just as I was getting going here. I feel frustrated at times like that, when I think I'm going to have some uninterrupted time to myself and she wakes up, wants to climb up on the kitchen counter, take a bath, punch the keys on the computer, touch the apple on the computer, play with black indelible marking pens, eat something, go potty, smash the kitty, cry cause the kitty scratched her, get a boo-boo bunny, and play. I have a very hard time keeping a lid on the feelings. I look at her and I melt. That doesn't help. Then God help Bob if he should ask me what time it is, or where he left his glasses. It makes me furious to have to think of anyone else's needs or wants if I am not being diligent about seeing that my own needs and wants are being met as well. I grit my teeth so hard that I'm surprised they don't just crumble out of my gums afterwards. I also like to smash the mail around making loud noises, or throw the newspaper. I try to pick things that don't entail much clean-up, because then I defeat myself in my own anger. Yelling is good, growling better. I'd like to bite someone.

The payoffs for living with people that you love are enormous — but just where are women supposed to discharge of or dispose of the free-floating rage? The best place for me to do this has always been groups of women where we can discuss our lives freely, i.e. a good twelve-step meeting where they haven't forgotten the principals so vital to our survival and growth — honesty and open-mindedness. It's a powerful tool to discharge the pent up frustrations in our daily lives. If we live with others we have to learn how to not lose ourselves, sell ourselves out, in the course of everyday living. If we live alone we sometimes have to learn how to deal with the loneliness. Each path has rewards.

Anyway, for me the experience of talking about the things I am working on in my daily life, or what's driving me crazy (the kiddie pizza parlor) really puts it all in perspective. It helps me when I know that I am not the only one. It really helps me when I can laugh and hear the laughter of identification from others. It helps me ease into the experience of being a human being — something that does not come easily or naturally

132

for me. Howling laughter is the best for me. Coyote Woman wakes up from a disturbing dream and finds she has become a mother...

(I find myself with a little problem here. I can't stop writing because the disc I am trying to save this on is full. I can't close the document. Bob's asleep and I don't do instruction books. I have to just keep on writing until he wakes up. It's the disadvantage to the learn-as-you-go method of computer usage.)

The desert is full of crows that are crazier than pet coons. I can hear them outside the office window right now yelling at each other. I see a crow starkly flying against the ultra-blue desert sky and think that I cannot ever leave this barrenness and it's hard-edged beauty.

How will I leave these haunted mesas where I lived before and hope I do not have to live again? Life is funny that way, the opposite ends of the same feeling, all at the same time.

November 20, 1990

Here it is, a crisp high desert morning. Heavy coat worn over pajama top to take Sasha to pre-school. I often wander around in pieces and parts of my sleeping garb throughout the entire day. It's one of the secrets of my creative output. I don't waste time getting dressed in the morning.

I have been cutting and pasting to get a mock-up of my ad. My article for Athena is done. I'm waiting for the proof sheet from the lab in Las Vegas. The machine is moving forward. I plan on submitting the piece to several different publications.

I was able to paint yesterday on "El Dia de los Muertos" while my wonderful student, Shelby was here. This morning I'm going to go down to the library to look for a picture of a dog skeleton to complete the composition. It's a haunting painting with all my dead people. The self-portrait part has a very surreal quality. It's so solid — so grounded and earthy amidst the dead ones.

The most important thing, though, is that I was able to paint again. It's such a juggling act to write, to paint, to go to the gym, to look after Sasha, give love and attention to Bob, and dig out from under the mountain of dishes and diapers. I am angry so much of the time. I don't like to do things around the house. When I am alone I keep everything ship-shape. You can't do that with three grown-ups and a two-and-a-half-year-old. I get angry when they leave things for me to do. I usually tell them, which of course makes me look like a big, complaining bitch. I don't want to pick up one sock or wash one glass.

I go through periods when it's hard to let people know how I feel, because I don't think they're going to want me around. I force myself to do it again and again because if I don't, I don't like me. The price is much too high. So I risk their disapproval and often get it. I have my own self-respect, but acquiring the ability to feel that has meant that I must really exert myself. Living on self-validation and spiritual validation has been a hard-won lesson. I still have to push myself to it.

November 25, 1990

We have just lived through a horrendous Thanksgiving that reminded me why I have made a point to never be within ten miles of my family on a holiday. I had everything ready to cook and the big bird was in the oven when we decided to go out for a short hike in the desert. We stopped at the Acer's home and had a wonderful impromptu visit — the kind of thing that makes it nice living in a small town. There was a power outage and we decided to walk back to see how our dinner was doing.

It was autumn out — a cold wind snapped around us as we began to hike down the dirt road that snakes out of sight between our houses. Bob put Sasha up on his shoulders and we began to cut across the rugged desert to speed up the trip a little. I bent to pick up one of the many Indian hand tools that are to be found strewn on the ground throughout the area. As I examined the chipped edges all around — it looked like a scraping tool, we heard the sound of several sirens coming from a long way off. We picked our way around the cactus joking that perhaps they were coming to rescue our turkey or maybe even my mother. It wasn't long before it became apparent that they were in fact coming to our house. I began to run as best I could. The desert is full of quite a few more obstacles and growing things than the uninitiated would imagine.

The panic didn't really set in for a while this time as often happens when you have expected someone to die over and over again, only to have them call you a few hours later and ask you to bring them some gum or their ballet shoes or something. Mom had passed out on the john, bashed her head and bled profusely. We had a house guest, Larry, who was smart enough to get in there and see if she was all right. She had then fallen out of her bed as he went to call for help. When I got to her she was being surrounded by paramedics, firemen, police. She was grey, grey, grey of the worst hue. Her mouth was ringed by blood, which was spattered around the room. Once again, she looked as if she were about to die. I went on the now familiar trip to the hospital in the front seat of the ambulance.

After awhile I called Bob to come pick me up so I could escape the crowded waiting room full of sad, ashen faces, one of which was mine. How many years have I been coming to my parents' deathbeds and how long will this go on? I am depleted, exhausted, angry. All I want to do is to pack up my studio and go home to Santa Fe with Bob and Sasha. I am dying to get out of here and I pray I don't stress myself out so much that it could become a reality. I know that sounds overly-dramatic, but my spirit doesn't do well in incarceration. I just can't resolve the situation of what to do with my mother who has the constitution and the stubbornness of a mule. I simply cannot just dump her alone unless things get too obviously bad. I'm on hold waiting for more intuitive information from inside of myself. Right now I am only in utter chaos and confusion, but I do know how to do that.

November 30, 1990

I can only steal a few minutes here and there to work. Fortunately the Mac is easy-in, easy-out. This morning I was dreaming of Bird People all dancing and making bird calls in a circle. I had wings and I was dancing in front of them.

My article and ad are almost ready to go. That's my priority right now, just to get them where they're supposed to be when they're supposed to be there.

Chapter 18

THE GHOST DANCE

Warrior Woman goes to Tucson . . . Camp Fort Beale . . .
Coyote Woman comes to take me away . . .

December 8, 1990

Drove in late last night from Tucson. We bought a house there. It looks like it will be okay, certainly on a temporary basis. I just need a miracle to keep from falling apart. I am depleted but putting one foot in front of the other.

I am more and more wired with every few days that pass. I think I am letting go of my mom and many other subterranean structures. Rather than harping on how exhausted I am, I am going to make a giant effort to remember that I will have all the energy that I need to do whatever I will have to do in the coming months. Astrologically it's a time for goodbyes. I hope so. I hope soon.

December 12, 1990

I'm still in this bizarre no-sleep mode. Two nights ago I had a vision of my last big painting to do in Kingman. I was lying in bed trancing when a whole troupe of ghost dancers came stamping into my inner field of vision. The dancers entered from the right, chanting and stamping slowly but steadily. I knew it was another phone call from people who lived here long ago, people who have left their imprint and their heartbreak here in Kingman. The Ghost Dancers. They are still here, moving with their determination and their pain and their hope.

I want to paint their dance in 6'x8' format — something easy to move. I'm going to see if I can locate the supplies and have them shipped today. No wonder I can't sleep. I have work to do and it has to dry before we leave the confusing and sometimes dark vortex of Kingman.

December 19, 1990

Things are progressing well in our move to Tucson. Each time I go I like it more and look forward to going. The house is warm and inviting. There isn't a separate studio. I'll paint in the middle of the living room again. I did okay with that in Los Angeles. We'll rip out a wall and add some French doors for light and air. The room will be spectacular to work in.

The giant canvas has arrived from Santa Fe where I have most of my supplies shipped from. It's big. I mean eight feet is big. I thought for awhile that it might be too much to crate it when it's done, but I think I will simply paint it and then take it off the bars — something I don't usually do, but the size demands it. I don't want to wait until we get to Tucson to paint the Ghost Dance. It's the last piece in my cycle of work here in Kingman. I'll stretch it after Christmas and get to work on it before New Year's. This month there are two full moons. One full moon is on December 31, so I want to begin this monster painting before then.

Teaching has many advantages. One of the disadvantages is that I think about leaving my students when I move. There are two very special, very dear people I have been working with most of the time I have been here, Sharon and Shelby. Painting with them has been beautiful for me, and I am going to miss them terribly. When we looked at the new house I found myself thinking about where Shelby could stay when she comes. I cry when I think about leaving her. She is an intelligent and devoted artist at age ten, and good company as well. I dread leaving her sunny face. Sharon's imagination flows like a river of images, which happens for a fortunate few. We have traded art lessons for therapy with enormous benefit to me. There are things about Kingman that I will miss. Even though I want to go badly and soon, there will be tears.

December 27, 1990

I have been down the chute and into oblivion since I wrote my entry ten days ago. My exhaustion level has pushed me to the brink, and I became unable to work. The deaths and resurrections of my father and mother over the last two years have taken a serious toll on me and sometimes I fear for my health. I can't remember the last time I had any fun.

I started to stretch the canvas today for my last Kingman painting, the "Ghost Dance." One of the crossbars split, so I'm on hold, seeing if the local lumber yard can duplicate the bars that I otherwise have to have shipped at great expense and with delay from Santa Fe. I need to start that piece before the full moon on the 31st — before I close the doors down on the year 1990. There is tremendous joy and adventure for me in my painting even as I move through the most difficult passages of my life — as this doorway surely has been. The stretcher bars are standing assembled and upright in my room, like a giant skeleton. Even without the canvas stretched over the bones I get the same thrill of the chase as I gaze into the empty space. It's a big country to explore, a 6' x 8' expanse of nothing. I hope they can replicate the crossbar tomorrow because I can't wait to get at it. I've got one pint of energy left and I want to invest it in art. Art and sex, maybe. I wonder if I can stay awake long enough...

WARRIOR WOMAN

The new doberman, Belle, is asleep next to me with her beauteous brown head draped over the roll of canvas. Chile, the grande dame, is zonked out right behind my chair. Dogs and cats love to be right next to artists and writers when we work. Must be some positive ions pouring out of me — rather than the seemingly unending screaming I've been doing for the last few weeks. Feels heavenly to sit here again and listen to myself. It seems long — too long — since I have had the pleasure.

January 1, 1991

A new year. I won't miss the last one much. I feel great optimism looking towards 1991 and life in a new place, Tucson.

Started the "Ghost Dance" painting on December 30th. It's a wall of dancers — people who used to live here or passed through long ago. They are dancing still, in another world. Some of them I have seen before, but most are new. They want the harmony, balance, and beauty restored to the land, especially right here in Kingman. Tomorrow is the full moon, and their dance is well under way.

I have buried my smoky quartz crystals out in the desert for a few days to discharge all the cosmic crud they have been filtering. All the negativity is draining into the vast, lonely sands. I will dig them up soon to put them back to work.

As part of my ritualistic entry into 1991 I plan on painting when I am through writing. It was important to start this last big piece here in Kingman, where I got the messages, before the end of 1990, before the last full moon of the year. The painting lends some resolution to the pull that brought me here to this stagnant place. I am sure that I was living here before. Kingman is a cauldron of grief for me, and I look forward to leaving. Painting helps the time go by faster and with more meaning. I came here to work some things out, some from this lifetime and some from another life, no doubt. I came here to paint and write and I have done so. I have completed a mind-boggling amount of work as well as nearly completing my book. I can't wait to get out of the land of the dead.

January 10, 1991

More discussion on how to publish my book. Well, in my characteristic way, I've sent ads winging their way across the country, out into the universe, soaring into the galaxy, and I haven't a clue as to how I am actually going to publish The Thing. Commitment first, action follows.

I have much conflict over putting this into print. I look over certain parts and I want to throw up. Then I remember how I combed the shelves at bookstores, libraries, friends houses, looking for material written by other outsider-types — a vulture looking for fresh meat. I needed to know that there were/are other people who have had the calling to do life in a different way — listening only to the inner command. At the end of it all it doesn't matter one iota whether this is written perfectly, or even well. It's just another drumbeat in the orchestra of all life. It's the drum that is beating hard and fast, like the pounding of a baby's heart. Insistent. Strong. Vulnerable, too. Self-consciousness becomes beside the point.

I have been working hard on the "Ghost Dance," trying to work something out from the inside. I'm just past the stage where I hate it, but not yet into the part where I love it. Which parts are real, which are spirits, which are dreams? It's all the same to me. It's big, and they're dancing in my bedroom.

I spent time looking at it, some time standing on a table to paint, some time lying on the floor with Belle the Dog stomping over me, careening dangerously near my gooey palette.

Without asking me, today Bob volunteered me to do some workshops with him. My brain has been running at double speed since then designing the structure of what I'll do — what I like to do myself, choosing music, providing the arena in which to move — to dance. At first it sounded awful and then it sounded like a) a whole bunch of fun, b) gratifying, and c) very effective. The work I've done since I started this journal is coming full circle, working again using art, dance, writing, screaming, etc. with other people. That's appropriate as this five year cycle of intense growth and transformation is coming to a close. Into the fire with the phoenix...

January 25, 1991

I resemble a volcano spewing hot lava all over the house. I am mad as hell all the time. I feel repulsive, unlovable and furious. I asked my brother why he thought I might be so bursting with rage. "How about the whole situation? Living here, taking care of your mother, your life totally uprooted and centered around her needs." Ahh-hah. I was looking for something else, like maybe terminal p.m.s (two or three months?)... the new loco-bitch, Belle... a blamable reason, a way to dismiss it all.

Bob got me to one side to talk to me about my anger. "You've got to do something about it. You're angry all the time." Well, where do you dispose of this stinking toxic waste? Upon your child? Your husband? Yourself? Turn it inward? There's always cancer. No simple answers come — until a little later...

The truth is that I'm in a situation where it is appropriate to be angry — real angry. I need to be angry until I can take better care of myself. I need to stay steamed until I can get what it is that I need. Even though my anger is frightening to the people around me, they can handle it. My daughter can handle it, too. How else is she going to learn how to get angry and what to do with it? I sure didn't learn it in my family. They got angry, but nothing got changed. It's the unexpressed anger that's the killer of love for me. I'm just angry. Things need to change.

Tonight Sasha was needing some time and attention. She wanted to get out her paints. I'm not a spectator at heart, so I set up the double-sided table easel in the kitchen. I got out her finger paints and some brushes. Then I got out some paints for me and took up one of her stubby little-people type brushes. It felt good in my hands — sturdy, like a sure-footed little mule.

Sasha was thrilled that I was there painting with her. It solved the dilemma of just sitting and watching, which is hard for me to do — to sit still, not participating. Her remarks and comments took on a new dimension. I was there, but not watching her work. It left her independent, but close. She was talking to me while she worked — "I'm not done... I'm done... I wike my painting... Are you done?... Can I have another brush, Mama?... I wike red."

Well, Mama liked red, too! Out came the kind of painting at it's purest that really makes me feel connected to my art. RED! A wide-mouthed, screaming woman, radiating anger. It was magnificent! It just poured right out of me — the Cosmic Scream. "Help! Help!," she blurted out onto the paper. She was electrified with her rage. Something perhaps appropriate for a new generation of Hallmark cards? I mean it really is. If you received that in the mail, there would be no need for words inside the card. I got it all out on that newsprint and left it sitting on the kitchen table like a billboard to let everyone know just where I'm at. I feel a need to take the lid off the pain, the tension, the disappointment. Shortly after, there was a tiny "I'm done." piped around the corner. "Can I have a cookie, Mama?" Yes. I'll be glad to get you a cookie.

February 2, 1991

I'm almost alone, and what a relief it is! I often wish it was just Bob, me, and Sasha in the house alone, like a tiny little tribal unit, but we have been six and seven for a very long time now.

Preparations continue for our move to Tucson. I will be back painting in the middle of the living room. At first it seemed sad, and then I remembered all the years I spent working in my studio in Los Angeles that way, right in the middle of the main thoroughfare where I lived. I painted some of my best work there, and plenty of it. Somehow the thought of being where the dreaded television set, the bane of my existence, would be prattling on all the time sounded terrible. But that's the way I arranged it before — my painting right in the middle of the family living area, and it was good for me. I never produced more work than at that time. I just have to turn off the TV.

I have not completed the "Ghost Dance," but plan to do so before we move. It just feels important to complete the cycle of Kingman-inspired work in Kingman. It's almost impossible to regain the momentum after a cycle of work has been disrupted, particularly by something so unsettling as a move.

February 6, 1991

The "Ghost Dance" is finished. My room is filled with eleven dancers of varying degrees of membership in the known human race. They are in a trance, a dancing trance, with the purpose of wiping the intruding whites off the face of the earth, restoring the game, especially the buffalo, to the land, and reviving all their dead ancestors.

It seems so clear, insane-sounding, but clear — that since I have been in Kingman I have been receiving messages from the people who lived here long ago. Such a sad and painful place. It has been full of grieving for me, and apparently for many, many others. The Indians were imprisoned here. Broken. Everywhere you step you can feel their pain still oozing out of the land. As I look out of the window in back of my computer there is a palpable sense of sadness, disappointment. Long shadows flit across the empty land. It matches where I am emotionally. There is great, rich beauty, but it aches.

There is a sadness, too, in leaving such a place. I am sorry I could not do more here. I have painted and painted and painted. Written, too. But the loneliness! And only a few other isolated souls to share it with. I have done what I wanted to do in coming to this wasteland, and in that way Kingman has been good for me.

I'm going to Tucson to jump back into the river of life, distracted from the minute and painful inner workings of my Self. In many ways it will be a relief. The inner struggle becomes all-encompassing, engulfing, finally I am swallowed completely — lost to life. Every few years I have to come out. In Kingman, I find myself left with only the inner resources. Unless I want to play softball.

WARRIOR WOMAN

Still, it is such a pleasure to leave the door open and let the desert wind fly through the house and swirl around me, sometimes hot enough to melt you, sometimes bitingly cold. It's like being able to work out in the yucca, the Spanish bayonet, the beaver-tail. And the scorpions, tarantulas and coyotes. I will miss it, but I can't wait to get out of here.

Later...

Tonight I took a bath in the hottest water I could squeeze out of the hot water heater. Afterwards, sweating, I went for one of those incredible desert night walks. There were stars everywhere — on my hands, my feet, in my hair streaming out into the wind. The Milky Way came down and wrapped itself around me and I shimmered down the blackening road. Coyotes sang their insane and reedy opera in the darkness nearby. I could see the mesas more and more clearly as I walked out into the sueded night. Cassiopeia was doing a shoulder-stand on the big black mesa. The Pleiades were holding their nightly party, Orion twinkled a greeting. The Big Dipper has moved a long way away from where it was a few months ago — perhaps a quarter of the way across the sky. I gazed out long into the vibrant darkness that is peculiar, and I mean peculiar, to the desert. The scrub begins to undulate when you look long upon it. The desert wiggles and writhes when you are out walking alone in it at night, full moon or none. But I walked with Belle, the hound from hell, and I fear no man as we perambulate through the dark, drinking it all in — the desert, the delicious solitude. The desert ate us, and no-one knew where we were.

There is nothing here but the beautiful and mercurial, the moody land, and whatever one creates for oneself.

February 8, 1991

Went to see *Dances With Wolves* for the second time this evening. I found it even more affecting the second time around. I appreciated the casting choice of the female lead, Stands With a Fist. She was a good actress, we had not seen her in anything before, and she wasn't one of the legion of Hollywood blondes with boobs that grow so plentifully in Los Angeles.

I think about the War in the Gulf at night and I can't sleep. It brings back waves of nausea like I experienced as one by one my friends went off to Viet Nam. It was even more nauseating when the beautiful and once-whole young men came staggering back broken, twisted, unable to be reached, drug-addicted and alcohol-ravaged. It may well be a necessary evil, our participation in the war

— human beings have such a streak of violence and cruelty — but I cannot help but wonder, do people think this through? Do you really send idealistic young people into chemical weaponry wielded by such an obvious psychopath?

In looking at the politicians of the day, I am often reminded how the field of politics magnetizes charismatic psychopaths, puts them in office, puts the reins of power right into their carefully-posed open hands. They look you right in the eye and smile! How grateful I am that I do not have a son to be a pawn in the hands of men who do not know them or love them. I wonder at the foolishness of women now who, to prove their so-called equality with men, would voluntarily put themselves in the hands of such people and women-haters! Go to the war, into combat? War. It's a disease — unless one is defending one's own homeland. That's not what they say, but sometimes in life you have to turn off the volume and watch the action to find out what's really going on.

February 9, 1991

I bought the book, *Meditations for Women Who Do Too Much*, by Anne Wilson Schaef. It looks very good. I don't have time to read it. Every time I pick it up, five or six more days have passed.

February 11, 1991

Went out to Camp Fort Beale today with some friends. We took drums and rattles and scoured the land rounding up lost spirits who wanted to come with us. We took them all to the flagpole and lit a tiny fire that burned my hand. The old ones were mad as hell out there and didn't care if we were do-gooder Anglos or just more bastards. Anyway, I looked up the length of the flagpole and saw all these wiggly beings writhing up and away like tadpoles, as fast as can be.

For hours afterwards I was assaulted from the unseen plane, darkness washing all around me. It happens sometimes when I go to places that have been tainted by evil acts. I was huddled down inside of myself trying to make a smaller target when I detected a motion like a scared cat jumping sideways. I looked up and saw Coyote Woman dancing towards me. She held a stick high above her head and shouted.

She danced all around me and the evil things scattered. Only a trickster would have fought and won that kind of battle so easily. "What are you doing here?" I asked. "I've come to get you out of here. You've done what you were supposed to do here and now I'm getting you the hell out of Kingman!" So I'm going to let her lead the way, knowing the path will fall off into the crack between the worlds behind us as we go.

April, 1991, Tucson, Arizona

Final note to the reader:

At the time of the editing of this book I find myself in a new life in Tucson. Since our decision to leave Kingman, we wanted nothing but to move home to Santa Fe, but were unable to do so due to my mother's failing lungs and heart. Upon unenthusiastically investigating Tucson as a possible place to live, every obstacle began to remove itself. Each seemingly closed door swung open wide of its own accord, drawing me southward. I feel once again as if I have been brought to this place by the same irresistible forces that have brought me to each new adventure and removed me from each experience when my work was done there.

I like Tucson very much. The spirits are strong here. They have not abandoned the area with the encroachment of civilization. It is rich with magic and mysticism. I feel at home here for now. I have opened my studio/gallery, started painting full blast, and have begun the next volume of my journal, *Coyote Woman*. I hope it doesn't take as long as this one to complete!

My dreams have been vivid in Tucson. I feel quite grounded. Rooted even. The whole tribe seems to be thriving. We are a tough stand of prickly pear cactus, bursting with yellow flowers. A coyote left its skull for me. Someone who travels between the worlds delivered it, with a little meat left on it. It's laughing a crazy laugh on my porch. I can hear it at night. It is spring in the desert.